# MATH PROBLEM SOLVING:
# BEGINNERS
# THROUGH GRADE 3

**James L. Overholt**
*California State University, Chico*

**Jane B. Rincon**
*Chico Unified School District*

**Constance A. Ryan**
*Gateway Montessori School*

**ALLYN AND BACON, INC.**
**Boston      London      Sydney      Toronto**

**Library of Congress Cataloging in Publication Data**

Overholt, James L.
    Math problem solving.

    Bibliography: p.
    Includes index.
    1. Problem solving.  2. Mathematics—Study and teaching
(Elementary).  I. Rincon, Jane B.  II. Ryan, Constance A.
III. Title.
QA63.O87   1985        372.7        84-6205
ISBN 0-205-08215-7


Printed in the United States of America

10 9 8 7 6 5 4 3 2 1    89 88 87 86 85 84

# Contents

# Preface

Story and word problems have long been considered the bridge that will help students learn how to solve everyday-life problems that involve mathematics. However, teaching children to solve such mathematical problems has at times been frustrating for teachers. Sometimes it seems as if students randomly select a numerical answer for a verbal problem, giving little attention to the actual problem situation or logic of the solution. This does not need to be the prevailing situation. Young children can and should begin to interpret and solve various types of story and word problems soon after they have learned to count with understanding. Therefore, substantial portions of our mathematics programs need to be designed to help children become better problem solvers.

This book* utilizes much of the available research information in a complete sequence of lessons that teachers of beginning students and those in grades 1, 2, and 3 can use to guide their students in solving mathematics story and word problems. The lessons for each grade level incorporate a major problem-solving process and one or more supporting techniques. Furthermore, the problem-solving lessons in this book have been classroom tested for practicality and statistical reliability. In all phases of this testing, the performance of the students indicated statistical significance in favor of the techniques and problems cited (see Chapter 6 for details).

The purposes of this book are (1) to provide teachers and/or parents with a method and the corresponding lessons for teaching mathematical problem solving to young students and (2) to provide the information to enable young students to become more proficient problem solvers.

ACKNOWLEDGMENTS We wish to thank the students, teachers, and administrators from the Chico Unified School District who assisted in teaching, testing, researching, and revising these problem-solving lessons. A special note of gratitude goes to

*A companion book, *Math Problem Solving for Grades 4 through 8,* is available from Allyn and Bacon, Inc., 7 Wells Ave., Newton, Massachusetts 02159.

the classes at Neal Dow, John McManus, Hooker Oak, and Jay Partridge schools who assisted with the initial field testing of these materials. With their assistance, it was determined that the teaching methods and the corresponding problems presented in this book can help students understand and solve mathematics story and word problems.

Appreciation is also extended to California State University, Chico. In addition, a special thank you to Kathleen Lewis, Shannon Horn, Barbara Cochran, and Claudia Vinsonhaler, who typed the original research manuscript; and to Susan Greco, Gloria Murray, Debbie Campbell, Pennie Morejohn, Nancy Hamilton, Susan Tanner, Lisa Martin, and Mary Dee Winslow, who completed the revised manuscript. We also thank Sandy Barnes and Ira Nelkin, who provided statistical and computer assistance.

Finally, the authors would like to dedicate this book to all who have provided encouragement, understanding, and patience. Jim Overholt praises the Lord for this successful undertaking and also sends a special note of love to Pat, Sara, and Dan. Connie Ryan says thank you to everyone, and Jane Rincon extends thanks to her family and friends.

# INTRODUCTION

Why should story and word problem-solving lessons be included in an already overcrowded curriculum? The answer relates to the fact that we want students to grow in their abilities for dealing with the many and varied types of problems that they will encounter in their daily lives. The types of story and word problems presented in this book can provide a beginning for young children; these problem-solving lessons can expose them to a variety of problem situations, cause them to use algorithms in meaningful ways, provide for drill in the associated mathematical processes, and help them to learn to attack problem situations in a logical manner. To summarize, this book is designed for teachers and/or parents who wish to help young children to understand and solve mathematics story and word problems.

The problem-solving lessons for beginners and grades 1, 2, and 3, are located in Chapters 2, 3, 4, and 5, respectively. It is suggested that the lessons be dealt with at the rate of one each week. However, it is possible to introduce two problem-solving lessons each week, thereby completing those for a particular grade in a shorter time period. At the onset the lessons may require as much as 30–45 minutes of class time; but as the students become familiar with the format and procedures, less time will be needed. The grade levels on the lessons are designated as follows:

B = Beginners (lessons for most kindergarteners and talented preschool students)

| = Grade One

∟ = Grade Two

⊔ = Grade Three

Each lesson makes use of a major problem-solving approach, which can be used with any story or word problem, and one or more of a series of supporting techniques. Once formally introduced to the major approach, the children should work through each step; but after becoming familiar, they need to refer directly to the approach only as needed. Very briefly, the steps in this major problem-solving approach are:

1 Main Idea (In Your Own Words)

2 Question

3 Important Facts

4 Relationship Sentence (No Numbers)

5 Equation

6 Estimation

7 Computation

8 Answer Sentence

The supporting techniques include:

1 Using Mathematical Vocabulary

2 Finding Key Words and Phrases

3 Presenting Word Problems Orally

4 Problems Based on a Theme

5 Solving Problems with Pictures

6 Drawing Pictures to Solve Problems

7 Solving Problems with Diagrams

8 Drawing Diagrams of the Problems

9 Building Tables to Solve Problems

10 Solving Problems from a Graph

11 Writing Original Problems

12 Solving Two-Step Problems

13 Problems with Irrelevant Information

For complete information on how to use the major problem-solving approach and the supporting techniques, see Chapter 1. An index, which classifies the student lessons (from Chapters 2 through 5) according to grade level and the type of problem-solving technique being stressed, is located at the end of the book.

Understanding and solving math story and word problems is often difficult for young students and frustrating for teachers. However, if children are taught word problem-solving techniques and are provided with a sequence of lessons with which to practice, they will become better mathematical problem solvers. If the lessons provided in this book can help teachers and/or parents to help students to achieve these goals, then the authors' purposes will have been achieved.

# Chapter 1

# HELPING YOUNG CHILDREN TO UNDERSTAND AND SOLVE MATHEMATICS STORY AND WORD PROBLEMS

Children come to school with the ability to solve problems. In fact, during their everyday lives, most of them have already had to solve problems of many types. Despite this, teaching children to deal effectively with math story and word problems can be frustrating. It often seems as if students randomly select answers, or they become upset and simply quit altogether. When students react in this manner, teachers are often unsure how to help.

Before beginning a search for ways to successfully teach and learn skills for solving problems, it is necessary to define problem solving both generally and in relation to those terms that refer specifically to mathematical problem solving. In general, "problem solving" may be thought of as the process of applying previously learned rules to a situation that is new or different for the learner. In mathematics for young children, the most common means for portraying problem-solving situations are through the use of "story problems," "word problems," and "verbal problems." Because these terms are very similar, definitions of their use in this book are as follows:

Story problems: those mathematical problem situations that are presented orally.

Word problems: similar, or even the same, problems set forth in written or printed form.

Verbal problems: either story or word problems.

With these definitions as a focus, the authors of this book sought techniques that teachers could use effectively to help students become better at solving math story and word problems. We examined the available problem-solving research. On the basis of the research we selected, compiled, and adapted successful techniques for teaching mathematics problem solving. Then lesson plans were designed on the basis of these techniques (see Chapters 2 through 5). These lessons were then tried in classrooms, with the result that the students involved achieved at a significantly higher level than others who were not involved (see Chapter 6). Thus the lesson plans included in this book can provide students with both pertinent solution strategies and related math story and word problems for practice.

Kindergartners and talented preschool students who can accurately count objects and understand basic number concepts are ready to begin solving math story problems. The lessons prescribed for these young children (Chapter 2: Beginners Problem-Solving Lessons (Level B)) include making use of familiar, everyday situations, manipulative materials, and pictures or simple diagrams of the problem settings. The early lessons prepare these children for an introduction to the major problem-solving approach and a series of supporting techniques.

Students in Grades 1, 2, and 3 are verbally introduced to the major problem-solving approach during the first few lessons and then to the additional support techniques during ensuing lessons (see Chapters 3, 4, and 5). The major problem-solving approach provides students with a step-by-step method for attacking and working through the story and word problems. With young children, and initially with older students, it is expected that this approach will be completed orally. The major problem-solving approach also provides a framework for problem-solving diagnosis by the classroom teacher. For example:

*Problem*

David has 4 toy horses and John has 3 toy horses.

How many toy horses do they have altogether?

| |
|---|
| **Main Idea** *(in your own words)*<br>Some boys have toy horses. |
| **Question**<br>How many toy horses do they have together? |
| **Important Facts**<br>David has 4 horses.<br>John has 3 horses. |
| **Relationship Sentence\*** *(How will you do it?)*<br>The number of horses David has plus the number John has will be the total number of toy horses. |
| **Equation**<br>4 + 3 = __?__ |
| **Estimation**<br>4 + 3 is about _____. |
| **Computation**<br>4 + 3 = __7__ |
| **Answer Sentence**<br>Together the boys have 7 toy horses. |

*(\*Attempt to state the process without using numbers.)*

2

**MAJOR PROBLEM-SOLVING APPROACH**

Each step in the major problem-solving approach (see sample problem) has been found to be of assistance when solving mathematics story and word problems. Note that most of the steps are to be completed verbally. In this way, even very young children can be helped to begin thinking logically. The individual steps and their functions are described as follows:

1 *Main Idea.* This step requires the student to determine what the problem is about. It provides a basis upon which to start working on the problem.

2 *Question.* This step directs the student to look for what is being asked in the problem.

3 *Important Facts.* The student is required to note the important facts in the problem that he or she must use in order to solve it. This step helps the student disregard any unnecessary information or to identify any information that may be lacking.

4 *Relationship Sentence.* The student is asked to state verbally (preferably without the use of numbers) how to solve the problem. This step helps the student organize any thoughts about the problem, and select the computational operations to use. (Some primary teachers identify this step for their students as *How Will You Do It?*)

5 *Equation.* The important facts are put into a number sentence or algorithm based upon the relationship sentence.

6 *Estimation.* The student is called upon to make a reasonable "guess" as to what the answer will be before counting or computing it.

7 *Computation.* The student computes the answer and compares it with the estimated answer.

8 *Answer Sentence.* The student verbally states the computed answer in a complete sentence that answers the question in the problem.

When first working with the major problem-solving approach, the students should be required to work through (verbally) all steps. However, as the more able students become familiar with it, teachers may want to simply list the steps on a chart and have these students use the approach as a reference for getting started and working through the "tough spots" in any problem. Teachers, in turn, may utilize the steps as a diagnostic tool for determining exactly where in the process individual students are encountering difficulties.

Some students may resist working through each step because they can find the answers without doing so. The fact that they can determine solutions is commendable; however, they may not be attacking the problems in any sort of a logical manner. Thus while creative solutions are to be encouraged, the emphasis here is on the use of a logical approach that might be used with any problem. Insist, therefore, that they complete all steps for several lessons and on any problems thereafter when they encounter difficulties. In fact, during the early lessons, if some students tend to work ahead on problem pages without reviewing the steps, you may want to cut the pages into separate problems and give out only one portion at a time. This insistence upon completing each step helps them to learn the approach thoroughly before encountering more difficult problems. Finally, if a student should answer a problem incorrectly, be sure to review the steps with the child to determine where the error was made. In this way the children can be shown how the major problem-solving technique provides something to "fall back on" when they don't understand where they went wrong.

## SUPPORT TECHNIQUES

On the basis of research findings, the authors incorporated the following support techniques within the framework of the major problem-solving approach. The support techniques, each accompanied by a sample problem, leading questions to ask students, and other comments, are discussed next.

## A. Developing Mathematical Vocabulary (from Beginners, Lesson B-12)

Young children deal most effectively with story problem situations when they concern things the children know about. In this lesson the kindergarten children are shown picture rubbings of a leaf, a key, and a coin. They are told that they will be able to make some rubbings too, but first they are going to answer some questions. Then choose two children and give one five leaves and the other four leaves. Ask each child to count how many leaves he or she has. Now tell the children the following story problem:

Amy and Derek are going to make leaf rubbings.

Amy has 5 leaves. Derek has 4 leaves.

Who has *more* leaves?

Discuss the story problem with the children by asking them the following questions:

*Leaves.*

1 What is the story problem about?

*Who has more leaves?*

2 What do you need to find out?

*Amy has five leaves, and Derek has four leaves.*

3 What do you need to know to find out who has more leaves?

*By looking to see who has more; by matching; by counting.*

4 How will you find out who has the most leaves?

5 Compare the number of leaves each child has by matching. Ask Amy to put one of her leaves on the table. Ask Derek to put one of his leaves below Amy's leaf. Repeat this process until all the leaves have been matched one to one and Derek has no more leaves left.

Amy

Derek

**Amy has more leaves.**

6   Derek has no more leaves left, but Amy has one leaf left. Who has more leaves?

**One more leaf.**

7   How many more leaves does Derek need so that both he and Amy have an *equal* amount?

Complete one or two problems in this manner. Then see whether the students can solve similar problems when the teacher provides the necessary manipulative materials and reads the problems aloud but does not ask the leading questions. At the end of the lesson, help the children to make their leaf rubbings.

**B. Finding Key Words and Phrases (from Grade 1, Lesson 1-5)**

Jim cleaned out the junk room.

He found 3 footballs and 4 baseballs.

How many balls did Jim find altogether?

The teacher should help the students to "work through" this problem and perhaps another. In doing so, the steps of the major problem-solving approach as well as the key words should be noted. In such verbal problems the key words or phrases often indicate the type of computation needed. For example, the key word *left* usually indicates subtraction, *in all* generally suggests addition, *altogether* in most cases calls for addition. However, it must be noted that there are instances when the problem language is such that the key word actually calls for a different operation. (Such a problem, which indicates subtraction, is "John had 7 golf balls but lost 3. How many golf balls does he have altogether?") As long as this limitation is understood, the following questions, which focus on the major problem-solving approach and key words, may be asked to assist the students as they attempt to solve the problem noted above.

**Balls.**

1   What is the problem about?

**How many balls did Jim find altogether?**

2   What do you want to find out? What is the question?

**Jim found 3 footballs and 4 baseballs.**

3   What do you need to know?

**Add the number of footballs Jim found to the number of baseballs he found.**

4   Tell in your own words what you need to do to solve the problem.

5

*Addition.*

5   What operation will you use?

*Altogether.*

6   Is there any particular word in the problem that lets you know you must add to find your answer?

Why?

*Because the way "altogether" is used here means putting the two sets of balls together.*

You may also want to show ⚾⚾⚾ + ⚾⚾⚾⚾ = _____balls.

7   Write a number sentence for this problem on the blackboard: (3 + 4 = _____)

8   What do you think your answer will be? Will it be greater than or less than 4?

9   Add, using your number sentence. What is your answer?

10   What did you guess your answer would be? Is it the same?

*Jim has 7 balls altogether.*

11   Give your answer in a sentence.

    The continued use of questions such as these, which stress the steps of the major problem-solving approach together with the study of selected support techniques, will cause students to gain competence in problem solving. Thus as your students work through the sequence of lessons appropriate for them, they will become better problem solvers.

**C. Presenting Word Problems Orally (from Grade 2, Lesson ⌐-8)**

Often in daily life, problems are presented in verbal form. Thus students need to master the skills related to interpreting and solving these kinds of problems. In this instance a price list for student reference is also provided. At the onset it is suggested that problems be read aloud twice. Then, on the first reading, the children will:

1   Listen carefully to the problem to note the main idea.

2   Listen for the question.

On the second reading, the students will:

3   Determine the important facts in the problem.

4   State how they will solve the problem.

5   Find the price(s) of the musical instruments from the price list.

6   Compute their answer mentally.

7 Write only the answer on their paper.

**Drumsticks: $2 a pair**

**Sheet Music: 20¢ a sheet**

Terry bought 2 sheets of music.

How much money did Terry spend?

Read the problem aloud twice. After each reading, leading questions such as the following should be asked.

*Buying sheet music.*

1 What is the problem about?

*How much money did Terry spend?*

2 What is the question?

Reread the problem once again and ask the children:

*The price of one sheet of music and that Terry bought 2 sheets.*

3 What do you need to know to solve the problem?

*I will read it from the picture.*

4 How will you find out the price of one sheet of music?

*I will add the price of one sheet of music together twice; or I will multiply the price of one sheet of music by 2.*

5 Tell in your own words how you will solve this problem.

*20¢*

6 How much is one sheet of music?

*Terry spent 40¢ for sheet music.*

7 Do the addition (or multiplication) in your head and write only your answer on the paper.

As the students become familiar with the process, you may wish to discontinue the questioning process. However, if any student encounters difficulty, you should use questions such as these to locate the trouble spot.

**D. Problems Based on a Theme (from Grade 3, Lesson ⊔-7)**

Problem solving in daily life sometimes requires the solution of several problems related to the same issue or theme. In this lesson a series of questions are framed using the cost of going swimming (illustration provided with Lesson ⊔-7).

| AGE | PRICE |
| --- | --- |
| Over 15 | 75¢ |
| 11–15 | 50¢ |
| 5–10 | 25¢ |
| Under 5 | Free |

John had $1.

He went for a swim.

How much money does he have left?

It is suggested that this problem, and the others from this lesson, be presented orally. Read the problem aloud twice. After the first reading ask:

*John went swimming.*

1   What is the problem about?

*How much money did John have left after he went for a swim?*

2   What is the question?

Reread the problem again and ask the children to listen for the important facts necessary to solve the problem:

*How much money John had in the beginning and how much he paid to get into the swimming pool.*

3   What do you need to know to solve the problem?

*Subtract the price of a swim from the amount of money John had in the beginning.*

4   Tell in your own words what you need to do to solve the problem.

*50¢*

5   What price will John have to pay for a swim?

6   Do your subtraction in your head without writing anything on your paper.

7  Write only the answer on your paper.

*John has 50¢ left.*

8  Give your answer in a sentence.

Tell the children that you are going to read some more problems about the cost of going swimming and that they should use the picture to find out the prices. The first time you read each problem, they should listen to find out what the problem is about and what the question is. On the second reading, they should determine the important facts, decide how to solve the problem, mentally calculate the answer (if possible), and write an answer sentence on their papers.

**E. Solving Problems with Pictures (from Beginners, Lesson B-9)**

In this lesson the kindergarten children are provided with pictures appropriate for each problem they are asked to solve. Use the picture of the bees (picture provided with Lesson B-9) to aid the children as they attempt to solve this problem.

## Sample:

Tell the children the following story problem:

The queen bee scolded 4 bees for being lazy.

She scolded 4 more for eating too much honey.

How many bees did she scold altogether?

Discuss the story problem with the children by asking them the following questions:

*Bees.*

1  What is the story problem about?

*How many bees did the queen bee scold altogether?*

2  What do you need to find out?

*The queen bee scolded four bees for being lazy and four more bees for eating too much honey.*

3  What do you need to know to find out how many bees the queen bee scolded altogether?

*I will count all the bees in the picture.*

*Because the picture shows the four bees that were scolded for being lazy and the four bees that were scolded for eating too much honey.*

4  Look at your picture. How will you find out how many bees the queen bee scolded?

Why?

5  How many bees do you think were scolded altogether? Were more than four bees scolded?

6  Count to find out how many bees were scolded.

*Eight bees were scolded.*

7  How many bees were scolded?

8  Did anyone guess correctly?

Follow a similar procedure with the following five story problems. Talk about each picture first before solving the story problem. Use the major problem-solving approach if the children have difficulty in solving the problem. Let the children color in their pictures at the end of the lesson.

You may wish to complete another problem together so that the children may have more practice at using pictures to help find their solutions. Then see if they can figure out the remaining problems when you read them aloud. However, if they need help, continue to use the steps in the major problem-solving approach as a guide.

**F. Drawing Pictures to Solve Problems (from Beginners, Lesson B-15)**

In this lesson the children are told simple story problems that are based on everyday types of experiences. They are then to draw pictures (manipulatives may also be used initially) to represent the situation. One such story problem is:

Sally played marbles with her brother Tom.

She had 3 marbles in the beginning and she won 2 more.

How many marbles does Sally have now?

In this case the students are asked to draw 3 circles to represent the marbles Sally had initially and then 2 more circles to show how many she won. (OOO  OO) Then the story problem should be repeated, and the following types of questions should be asked:

*Marbles.*

1  What is the story problem about?

*How many marbles does Sally have now?*

2  What do we need to find out?

*Sally had 3 marbles and she won 2 more.*

3  What do we need to know in order to figure out how many marbles Sally has now?

4  Look at your picture. How can you use it to find out how many marbles Sally has now?

*I will count the number of marbles I have drawn altogether.*

Why?

*Because I drew the 3 marbles she had in the beginning and the 2 she won from Tom.*

*Four, five, six marbles.*

5  How many marbles do you think Sally has now?

6  Count to find out exactly how many marbles Sally has.

*Sally has 5 marbles.*

7  How many marbles does she have?

8  Did anyone guess the right answer?

Do several more problems of this type with the children and help them to draw their pictures so they accurately represent the problem situations. Talk about the fact that their drawings mean the same as the actual objects in the problems. This lesson, and others like it, will help students to begin to realize that what is real can be represented and that they can use these representations to help solve the related problems.

**G. Solving Problems with Diagrams (from Grade 1, Lesson I-13)**

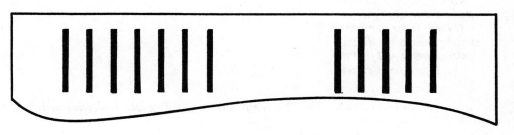

Tell the children to look at the top of their diagram sheet where they can see two groups of straight lines. Then, ask related questions such as:

*7*  1  How many straight lines are there in the first group?

*5*  2  How many straight lines are there in the second group?

*12*  3  How many straight lines are there altogether?

Next read the following problem slowly to the children:

I had 7 popsicle sticks.

The teacher gave me 5 more.

How many popsicle sticks do I have now?

Discuss the problem with the children by asking them the following questions:

*Popsicle sticks.*

1 What is the problem about?

*How many popsicle sticks do I have now?*

2 What is the question? What do you want to find out to solve the problem?

*I had 7 popsicle sticks and the teacher gave me 5 more.*

3 What do you need to know to solve the problem?

*Count or add the number of popsicle sticks I had in the beginning with the number of popsicle sticks the teacher gave me.*

4 Tell in your own words what you need to do to solve the problem.

*7 + 5 = _____*

5 Write a number sentence for this problem.

6 How could you use a diagram to find your answer?

*Each straight line represents a popsicle stick. The first group of 7 lines represents the 7 popsicle sticks I had in the beginning, and the second group of 5 straight lines represents the 5 popsicle sticks the teacher gave me. If I count the number of straight lines in the diagram altogether, I will find the answer.*

7 What do you think your answer will be? Will it be less than or greater than 7?

8 Find your answer using the diagram.

9 What did you think your answer would be? Is it the same?

*I have 12 popsicle sticks now.*

10 How many popsicle sticks do you have now? Give your answer in a sentence.

Continue this procedure with the following problems. You may want to do one more together and then let the children do the last few problems on their own (after the problems have been read aloud to them). Encourage the children to use the diagrams to help them to solve the problems and to compute their answer by counting.

**H. Drawing Diagrams of Problems (from Grade 2, Lesson L-12)**

After the students have solved problems that had related diagrams accompanying them, they should learn to draw their own diagram representations. The candies in the problem that follows, for example, can be represented by circles.

Robin bought 3 packs of candy.

There were 6 candies in each pack.

How many candies did Robin buy altogether?

Discuss the problem with the children by asking them the following questions:

*Candies.*

1 What is the problem about?

*How many candies did Robin buy altogether?*

2 What is the question?

*Robin bought 3 packs of candy and there were 6 candies in each pack.*

3 What do you need to know to solve the problem?

4 Instead of drawing a picture about the problem, this time we will draw a diagram. Let a circle (○) represent a candy, and let a (_____) represent a pack.

*6*   How many circles will we draw for the first pack of candy?

*6*   How many circles will we draw for the second pack of candy?

*6*   How many circles will we draw for the third pack of candy?

*3*   Now draw a straight line under each pack of 6 candies. How many packs of 6 candies do we have?

| ○○○○○○ | ○○○○○○ | ○○○○○○ |
|---|---|---|
| 6 candies | 6 candies | 6 candies |
| 1 pack | 1 pack | 1 pack |

*Add the number of candies in a pack together 3 times; or multiply the number of candies in each pack by the number of packs; or simply count all of the candies.*

5 Tell in your own words what you need to do to solve the problem.

*Add the number of circles together; or multiply the number of packs times the number of candies in each pack; or count the circles.*

6 How will I use the diagram to solve the problem?

*Because there are 3 groups of 6 circles representing the 3 packs of 6 candies.*

Why?

$6 + 6 + 6 = \underline{\hspace{1cm}}$ *or*
$3 \times 6 = \underline{\hspace{1cm}}$

7  Write a number sentence for this problem.

8  What do you think your answer will be?

9  Find your answer using your diagram.

10  Compare your answer with your estimation.

*Robin bought 18 candies altogether.*

11  Give your answer in a sentence.

Have the students follow a similar procedure for the problems on the student page. Encourage them to draw a diagram to aid in the solution of each problem.

## I. Building Tables to Solve Problems (from Grade 2, Lesson L-13)

In this lesson the students will learn how to construct simple tables to aid in the solution of certain types of problems.

Initially, read the following problem slowly to the children:

Tom has 2 more brothers than John has.

How many brothers does Tom have?

Next ask questions based on the major problem-solving approach such as the following:

*Brothers.*

1  What is the problem about?

*How many brothers does Tom have?*

2  What is the question?

*How many brothers John has and that Tom has 2 more brothers than John.*

3  What do you need to know to solve the problem?

*I will add 2 to the number of brothers John has.*

4  Tell in your own words how you will solve the problem.

*No.*

5  Do you know the number of brothers John has?

*Tom would have 2 brothers.*

*Because Tom has 2 more brothers than John and 0 + 2 = 2.*

*Tom would have 3 brothers because 2 + 1 = 3.*

*Tom would have 4 brothers because 2 + 2 = 4.*

6　If John had no brothers, how many brothers would Tom have?

　　Why?

7　If John had 1 brother, how many brothers would Tom have?

8　If John had 2 brothers, how many brothers would Tom have?

9　We can write our answer to this problem in the form of a table. Write this table on the chalkboard with help from the children.

| *Number of Brothers John Has* | *Number of Brothers Tom Has* |
|---|---|
| 0 | 2 |
| 1 | 3 |
| 2 | 4 |
| 3 | 5 |
| 4 | 6 |
| 5 | 7 |

10　By reading information from our table we can state our answer in sentences as follows:

If John has no brothers, Tom has 2 brothers.

If John has 1 brother, Tom has 3 brothers.

If John has 2 brothers, Tom has 4 brothers.

If John has 3 brothers, Tom has 5 brothers.

If John has 4 brothers, Tom has 6 brothers.

If John has 5 brothers, Tom has 7 brothers.

Tom has between 2 and 7 brothers, since it is unlikely that John has more than 5 brothers.

　　Have the students follow a similar procedure for each of the problems in this lesson. Construct a table for each problem. You may wish to do another problem with the children if they have not had previous experience involving the use of tables.

**J. Solving Problems by Making a Graph (from Grade 1, Lesson I-12)**

Young children can learn to make simple graphs and solve problems that relate to them. Copies of the empty graph shown below (provided for Lesson I-12) should be distributed to each student.

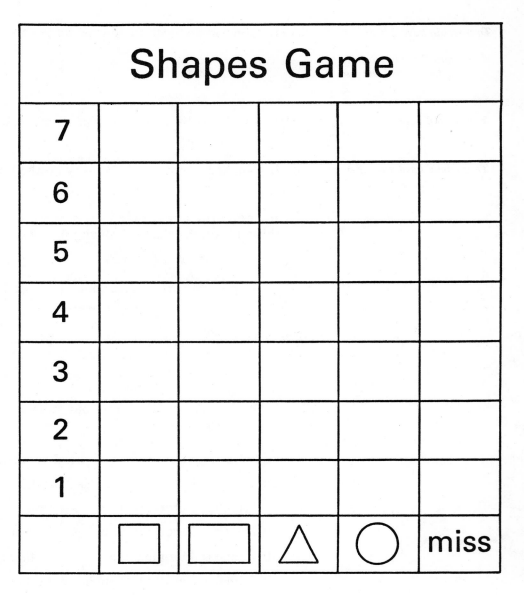

| | | | | | |
|---|---|---|---|---|---|
| **7** | | | | | |
| **6** | | | | | |
| **5** | | | | | |
| **4** | | | | | |
| **3** | | | | | |
| **2** | | | | | |
| **1** | | | | | |
| | □ | ▭ | △ | ○ | miss |

Provide chalk and a bean bag. Then take the children out into the school yard and draw the following shapes with chalk on the pavement:

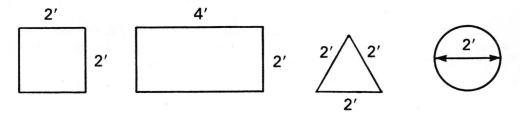

Draw a straight line between 8′ and 10′ from the shapes. You are now ready to start. The rules of the game are as follows:

1   Each child stands behind the line and throws the bean bag.

16

2 If the bean bag lands in a shape, the child records the score by making an "X" above the corresponding shape on his or her graph and gets another throw.

3 If the bean bag lands outside a shape or on a line, the child records a "miss" on his or her graph, and the next child has a turn.

Continue the game until someone gets 7 points in one shape or 7 points in all the shapes. Encourage the children to record all their scores. Someone who has 7 misses is eliminated from the game.

After the game, talk about what happened:

1 How many squares/rectangles/triangles/circles did you hit?

2 How many misses did you get?

3 Who hit the most squares?

4 What shape was the easiest to hit?

Then generate a story problem from the children's responses. Use a child's graph while telling the story problem. For example:

> Let's look at Regina's graph.
>
> She hit the square 5 times.
>
> She hit the rectangle 3 times.
>
> How many more times did she hit the square?

Finally, discuss the story problem with the children using the steps of the major problem-solving approach. Note specifically the main idea, question, important facts, etc. (The steps of this approach are outlined at the beginning of this chapter.) Continue this procedure of generating story problems from the children's graphs. Encourage them to use their graphs to solve the story problems.

**K. Composing Original Problems (from Beginners, Lesson B-8)**

The basis for this lesson is that of digging in a garden and collecting various items from the dig (worms, stones, etc.). Begin by taking a small group of children and the needed materials (shovels, collecting jars, magnifying glass, etc.) to the digging area. Then let them dig away, and encourage them to save what they find in the earth. Get them to put the worms, insects, and other things that they find in the jar. They can look at the worms through a magnifying glass.

Once they have gathered their findings, ask the children questions such as:

1 What did you find?

2  How many worms/stones/etc. did you find? (If necessary, help children count their findings.)

3  What do they look like?

4  What color are they?

*They crawl about.*  5  How do worms move about?

*In the ground.*  6  Where do worms live?

Next devise a story about the experience to give them the idea, such as:

> Erin found 2 worms.
>
> Jeremy found 3 worms.
>
> Who found more worms?

Can anyone else tell a story problem about digging? Help the children if necessary. For example:

*2 stones.*  1  Michelle, what did you find?

*Andy found 5 stones.*  2  Did anyone else find stones?

3  Tell me a story problem about the stones you and Andy found.

> Michelle found 2 stones.
>
> Andy found 5 stones.
>
> How many stones were found in all?

Repeat the children's story problems and solve them using the materials that they found. If the children have any difficulty in solving the problems, use the major problem-solving steps (see Chapter 1 for details) to help them work through the "tough spots."

## L. Solving Two-Step Problems (from Grade 2, Lesson L-15)

Solving word problems with more than one step can be confusing for students. However, the major problem-solving approach can be used quite effectively in such situations. For example, look at the picture provided and read the following problem slowly with the students:

> Jane has 4 kites.
>
> Ellen has twice as many.
>
> How many kites do they have altogether?

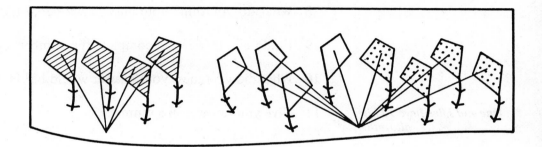

Discuss the problem with the children by asking them the following questions:

*Kites.*

1  What is the problem about?

*How many kites do Jane and Ellen have altogether?*

2  What is the question?

3  Look at the picture.

*3*

How many groups of kites are there?

*4*

How many kites are in each group?

The first group shows the 4 kites Jane has.

The other two groups show the kites Ellen has.

*Jane has 4 kites and Ellen has twice as many.*

4  What do you need to know to solve the problem?

*I will multiply the number of kites Jane has by 2 to get Ellen's total and then add the number of kites Jane has to that answer; or I will add the number of kites Jane has together 3 times; or I will count Ellen's kites and add them to the 4 that Jane has.*

5  How will you solve the problem? What will you do to solve the problem?

*2 × 4 = _____*
*+ 4 = _____*
*or 4 + 4 + 4 = _____*
*or 8 + 4 = _____*

6  Write a number sentence for this problem.

*I will count all the kites in the picture.*

7  How could you use your picture to find the answer to the problem?

*Because the picture shows the number of kites Jane has and the number of kites Ellen has.*

Why?

8 What do you think your answer will be? Will it be greater or less than 8?

9 Find your answer and complete the number sentence.

10 What did you guess your answer would be? Is it the same?

*Jane and Ellen have 12 kites altogether.*

11 Give your answer in a sentence.

Follow a similar procedure for the other two-step problems. Help the students to determine what the two steps are and specifically what information relates to each.

## M. Problems with Unnecessary Information (from Grade 3, Lesson ⊔-28)

Many problems from everyday life contain extra or unnecessary information. Consequently, these word and story problem-solving materials deal with such situations beginning in Grades 2 and 3. In this Grade 3 problem we have more prices than we need.

> Sam went to the store to buy some groceries. Packages of cheese were $2 each, rice was $1 a package, and coffee was $5 a jar. Sam bought 2 jars of coffee and a package of cheese. How much money did he spend?

When attempting to find a solution, the major problem-solving technique can be utilized as follows:

*Buying groceries.*

1 What is the problem about?

*How much money did Sam spend for the groceries?*

2 What question is asked?

*Sam bought 2 jars of coffee and a package of cheese; also, cheese was $2 per package and coffee was $5 per jar.*

3 What are the important facts?

*No.*

It also says in the problem that rice was $1 a package. Do you need to know the price of rice?

*Because Sam didn't buy any rice.*

Why not?

Good! Many problems have extra or unnecessary information like this. I'm happy that you discovered that you didn't need to know about the rice.

*I will add up the price of a package of cheese and the price of 2 jars of coffee, and that will be the total cost.*

4 Give a relationship sentence. Tell how you will use what you know about the cheese and coffee to solve this problem.

$2 + $5 + $5 = _____

5  Write the number sentence for this problem.

6  Will your answer be more or less than $10?

7  Add and find your answer.

*Sam spent $12 for a package of cheese and 2 jars of coffee.*

8  Give your answer in a complete sentence.

When students frequently encounter problems like these, with extra information, they will begin to deal with them quite effectively. This skill should then carry over into everyday life, where many problems have information that is not pertinent to their solutions.

## READING SKILLS AND THE MAJOR PROBLEM-SOLVING APPROACH

It should be noted that the major problem-solving approach used in nearly all of the lessons in this book teaches reading analysis at the same time that it teaches mathematics. Specifically, teachers have noted that both "finding the main idea" and "writing a complete answer sentence" carry over into reading and other subjects. "Finding the main idea" correlates with determining the major idea in descriptive subject matter; and once students become accustomed to "writing a complete answer sentence," they also do so when studying other subjects.

## MAINSTREAMING AND THE MAJOR APPROACH

A further point regarding the major problem-solving approach regards the use that some teachers have made of it with mainstreamed students. Because the approach can be used as a diagnostic tool, some teachers have noted that certain special students, even though they are generally working with problems at a lower grade level, are able to complete all but one or two of the steps without difficulty. Then by isolating the area(s) of special need and providing intensive remedial work on the step(s), the students are generally able to be successful with more advanced math story and word problems.

## CALCULATORS AND WORD PROBLEMS

Hand-held calculators, if properly used, can free students to deal with problems that might otherwise be too difficult for them. For example, if a first-grade child has a good understanding of place value and the process of addition, he or she can then use the calculator to complete computations involving the column addition of three-, four-, or even five-digit numbers.

Using calculators in this manner, however, does not imply that basic computation need not be learned and practiced. Rather, those students who have mastered the basics and have a thorough understanding of the processes involved may be encouraged to deal with more advanced story and word problems.

Teachers can provide for those students who are ready for such calculator use by doing one of two things. One possibility is to provide the students with lessons from an advanced level; Grade 1 students could do lessons from the third-grade chapter, for example. A second way to provide for such variance is to revise the existing word problems. For example, the second-grade problem that follows might be redone as noted:

*(Original)*          There are 8 oak trees and 6 pine trees growing in the garden. How many trees are there in all?

*(Revised)*          There are 8,247 oak trees and 6,175 pine trees growing in the forest. How many trees are there in all?

# Chapter 2

## BEGINNERS PROBLEM-SOLVING LESSONS: FOR MOST KINDERGARTENERS AND TALENTED PRESCHOOL CHILDREN
### (LEVEL B)

Many children come to kindergarten or preschool with a wide background of incidental experiences from which they have developed mathematical concepts. The lessons for this level are structured such that they will help to further develop and expand upon these understandings. The first lessons, which involve trading, sharing, and using drawings to represent situations, introduce young children to problem solving in a general manner. The elements of the major problem-solving approach are then introduced in lessons 3 through 10. (See Chapter 1 for a complete description of the major problem-solving approach and directions for its use.) In addition to this major approach, a series of supporting techniques (using pictures, concrete materials, drama, drawing, etc.) are also utilized in specific lessons in order to focus on the story problems and to help determine the answers. Finally, the children are helped to compose their own story problems.

The story problems in this chapter are based either on experiences that the children will have or on pictures that they can easily understand. The lessons often involve having the students make simple drawings of the situation. At first these pictures serve only as records, but gradually the students will begin to understand that real things can be represented. They are then on the road to exchanging manipulatives for other representational models in order to solve story problems.

The beginners chapter is arranged such that each lesson begins with plans for the teacher, including suggested questions and responses for a sample problem or situation. A copy of pictures needed or the student problem page follows. This arrangement provides the teacher with immediate access to Purposes, Materials, Directions, and Story Problems for the lesson as well as a copy of the student page. Any student pages or supplemental problem-solving aids (such as pictures or charts) in the chapter may be duplicated in quantities needed for the teacher's own classroom use.

Although the lessons have been designed primarily to develop problem-solving skills, they also provide counting and/or computation practice appropriate for children working at this level. Problems 1 and 2 for each lesson are quite easy, while Problems 3, 4, and 5 are more difficult. In addition, the lessons are sequenced so that those talented students who are able to do advanced work could be assigned the problems from Grade 1 (Level I).

# Lesson B-1  Introducing Problem Solving — Trading

**PURPOSES**

- To introduce children to problem solving by trading and encouraging them to trade.

- To talk about the trading (i.e., what they had in the beginning, what they traded, and what they have left now).

**MATERIALS NEEDED**

An envelope for each child containing either four crayons or four badges. Badges can be made by cutting out cardboard circles two to three inches in diameter and attaching an adhesive strip, or you may use the badges at the end of the lesson. (See Badges for Lesson B-1.) After the lesson the children can draw what they want on their badges.

Note: You may substitute similar items for the crayons and badges (e.g., pennies, balloons, candies, nuts, etc.). The items should be attractive to the children, they should be evenly matched so that the trading is not heavily one-sided, and the children should be allowed to keep what they receive.

**DIRECTIONS**

**1. Children Choose the Envelopes**

Put enough envelopes for each child in a Mystery Box. (A standard tissue box works well.) Each child then reaches in and takes out one envelope.

**2. Discussion**

Ask the children individually what they found when they opened their envelopes.

*4 crayons or 4 badges.*

1  What did you find inside your envelope?

*No. Some got crayons and others got badges.*

2  Did everybody get the same?

*Yes/no.*

3  Would you like to have crayons instead of badges?

**3. Teacher Demonstrates a Trade**

Begin the trading by saying:

I have 4 badges.

Will anyone give me a crayon for a badge?

If there are no traders, try:

Will anyone give me a crayon for 2 badges?

Trade with a volunteer. Then ask the children:

*You have 3 badges.*  1  How many badges do I have now?

*You have 1 crayon now.*  2  How many crayons do I have now?

Ask the volunteer:

*I have 3 crayons now.*  1  Lorraine, how many crayons do you have now?

*I have 1 badge now.*  2  How many badges do you have now?

## 4. Children Trade under Supervision

Tell the children:

What Lorraine and I did is called trading. You can trade with each other if you want. Who wants to trade?

While supervising each trade, ask the following questions:

*I have 4 crayons.*  1  What do you have?

*I want to trade a crayon for a badge.*  2  What do you want to trade?

3  Who will trade with Mary? (Mary and Mark trade with each other.)

*I have 3 crayons.*  4  How many crayons do you have now?

*I have 1 badge.*  5  How many badges do you have now?

If you feel that the children do not yet understand the concept of trading, continue to supervise. Tell them that once they trade something, they cannot take it back. They can trade back again only if the other person wants to as well. If a child does not want to trade, let the child keep what he or she was given in the beginning.

## 5. Children Trade by Themselves without Direct Supervision

Tell the children:

Now you can trade with each other on your own. If you want a crayon, you must find someone who wants a badge and will trade with you. If you want a badge, you need to look for someone who wants a crayon. If you need help, you can ask me.

**6. Discussion about the Trading**

Wait until everyone has finished trading and then talk about what happened. Begin by telling the children what you did:

> I started with four badges.
>
> I traded with Lorraine.
>
> I gave her one badge, and she gave me a crayon.
>
> Now I have three badges (count) and one crayon.

Ask each child the following questions:

1 What did you have in the beginning?

2 Who did you trade with?

3 What did you trade?

4 What do you have now?

Finish the lesson by getting the children to draw, color, and write on their badges. Listed below are variations to this lesson that you might like to try.

**VARIATIONS**

1 Use different items: beads, pennies, nuts, balloons, candies, etc.

2 Vary the number of items in each envelope; for example, put two badges in one envelope and four crayons in another to give a different trading ratio (one badge to two crayons).

3 Give everyone the same; for example, put three pennies and three peanuts in each envelope and encourage the children to trade.

Name_____

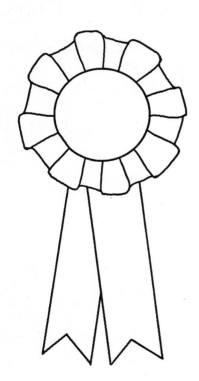

# Lesson B-2  Trading with Pictures

PURPOSES
- To talk about insects and trading.
- To develop story problems based on a trading experience.
- To use the major problem-solving approach to help solve the problems.

MATERIALS NEEDED
- Make copies of the pictures at the end of the lesson. (See Pictures for Lesson B-2.)
- Six envelopes and crayons.

DIRECTIONS

1. Getting Started

Working with a group of five children, cut out the pictures so that you have 12 of each kind, and put six of the same into each of two envelopes. (If the children can use scissors, have them cut out the pictures.) You will then have two envelopes with six butterflies, two with six bees, and two with six spiders.

2. Introduction

Everyone chooses an envelope without knowing which pictures are inside. Talk about what they found.

1  How many pictures did you get?

2  What are your pictures of?

*They are all insects.*

3  All the pictures are of butterflies, bees, or spiders. Do butterflies, bees, and spiders have anything in common?

4  Do you know of any other kinds of insects?

5  Where do insects live?

6  What is a butterfly called before it becomes a butterfly?

Let the children trade with each other.

3. Talk about the Trading

Ask the children the following questions:

1  What did you have in the beginning?

2   Who did you trade with?

3   What did you trade?

4   What do you have now?

**4. Story Problem**

Tell the children a story problem based on the trading experience. For example:

> I had 6 butterflies.
>
> I gave Jane 4 butterflies for 4 bees.
>
> How many butterflies do I have now?

**5. Use the Major Problem-Solving Approach**

Ask the children the following questions:

*Butterflies.*

1   What is the story problem about?

*How many butterflies the teacher has now.*

2   What do we want to find out?

*The teacher had 6 butterflies in the beginning, and he/she gave 4 to Jane.*

3   What do we need to know before we can solve the story problem?

*By taking 4 from 6; by counting.*

4   How will we find out how many butterflies I have now?

*One, two, three butterflies.*

5   How many butterflies do you think I have now?

6   Let's take four pictures away from the six.

*You have 2 butterflies now.*

7   How many butterflies do I have now?

8   Did anyone guess the correct answer?

At the end of the lesson, let the children color in their pictures. If they like, they could make a book of their insects by stapling their pictures together. Variations to this lesson are listed below.

**VARIATIONS**

1   Put four of each insect picture in every envelope and see if the children still trade with one another.

2   Use pictures of animals, birds, cars, spaceships, etc.

Name _____

# Lesson B-3    Solving Problems with Pictures

PURPOSES

- To expand the steps of the major problem-solving approach.

- To help the children to find the main idea in a story problem based on a picture.

- To help the children to determine what is wanted (i.e., the question). This step is being introduced here for the first time.

- To help the children to determine the important facts in a story problem.

MATERIALS NEEDED

- Duplicate the pictures of frogs and wigwams for each child. (See Pictures for Lesson B-3 at the end of the lesson.)

- Crayons.

DIRECTIONS

**1. Introduction and Discussion**

Give each child the picture of the frogs and tadpoles first and ask them the following questions:

*The frogs and tadpoles are swimming.*

1  What does this picture tell you?

*3*

2  How many frogs are there?

*4*

3  How many tadpoles are there?

*One is swimming, another is chasing a fly, and another is sitting on a log.*

4  What are the frogs doing?

*They are all swimming.*

5  What are the tadpoles doing?

*Frogs.*

6  What do tadpoles become when they grow up?

**2. Story Problem**

Ask the children to look at their picture and tell them the following story problem:

There are 3 frogs and 4 tadpoles in the picture.

How many more tadpoles are there than frogs?

**3. Major Problem-Solving Approach**

*Frogs and tadpoles.*

*How many more tadpoles are there than frogs?*

*There are 3 frogs and 4 tadpoles.*

*3*

*4*

Discuss the story problem with the children by asking them the following questions:

1  What is the story problem about?

2  What do we need to find out?

3  What do we need to know to find out how many more tadpoles there are than frogs? Can your picture help you?

If the last step is too difficult for the children, ask them to:

4  Count to see how many frogs are in the picture.

5  Count to see how many tadpoles are in the picture.

The emphasis of this lesson is on building and focusing on the language concepts necessary to solve story problems. At this stage, it is not necessary for the children to solve the story problem, but you may do so if you wish. Let the children color in their picture at the end of the lesson.

A similar procedure can be followed with the picture of wigwams. Listed below are story problems the children could talk about relating to the Indian and wigwam picture.

**STORY PROBLEMS**

1  Two Indians are sitting by the fire. Two more are going off to hunt. How many Indians are there altogether?

2  There are 5 wigwams and 4 Indians in the picture. How many more wigwams are there than Indians?

Name_____

Name_____

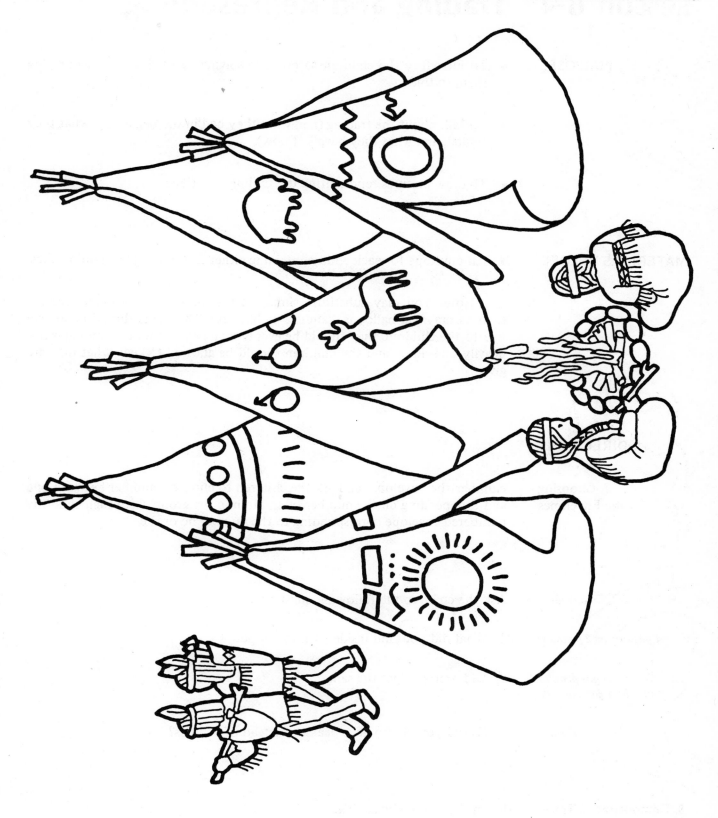

# Lesson B-4   Trading and Representing

**PURPOSES**
- To introduce the children to problem solving by trading and encouraging them to trade.

- To talk about the trading (i.e., what they had in the beginning, what they traded, and what they have left now).

- To draw pictures representing the trading experiences.

**MATERIALS NEEDED**
- An envelope for each child containing either four peanuts or two pennies.

   Note: You may substitute similar items for the pennies and peanuts, such as crayons, balloons, candies, badges, etc. The items should be attractive to the children, they should be evenly matched so that the trading is not heavily one-sided, and the children should be allowed to keep what they are given.

**DIRECTIONS**

**1. Choosing the Envelopes**

Number the envelopes and ask the children to choose a number between one and ?, depending on the number of children in the group. Give each child the numbered envelope corresponding to the number he or she chose.

**2. Discussion**

Ask the children the following questions:

*4 peanuts or 2 pennies.*

1 What did you find inside your envelope?

*No, some got pennies and others got peanuts.*

2 Did everyone get the same?

*Yes/no.*

3 Would you like to have peanuts instead of pennies?

**3. Demonstrate a Trade**

Begin the trading by saying:

I have 4 peanuts.

Will anyone give me a penny for 2 peanuts?

Trade with a volunteer. Then ask the children:

*You have 2 peanuts.*    1  How many peanuts do I have now?

*You have 1 penny.*    2  How many pennies do I have now?

Ask the volunteer:

*I have 1 penny.*    1  Larry, how many pennies do you have now?

*I have 2 peanuts.*    2  How many peanuts do you have now?

## 4. Children Trade under Supervision

Tell the children:

What Larry and I did is called trading. You can trade with each other if you like. Who wants to trade?

While supervising each trade, ask the following questions:

*I have 2 pennies.*    1  What do you have now?

*I want to trade a penny for 2 peanuts.*    2  What do you want to trade?

3  Who will trade with Alex? (Alex and Anne trade with each other.)

*I have 1 penny now.*    4  How many pennies do you have now?

*I have 2 peanuts now.*    5  How many peanuts do you have now?

The trading ratio need not necessarily be two peanuts = one penny. Let the children bargain with each other as long as no one is being forced to trade when they do not wish to participate. The children may trade back again if both parties agree. Continue to supervise the trading until the children are familiar with the procedure.

## 5. Children Trade by Themselves without Direct Supervision

Tell the children:

Now you can trade with each other on your own. If you want some peanuts, you have to find someone who wants a penny and will trade with you. If you want a penny, you need to find someone who will trade with you for some peanuts.

**6. Discussion about the Trading**

Wait until everyone has finished trading and then talk about what happened. Begin by telling the children what you did:

> I started with 4 peanuts.
>
> I traded with Larry.
>
> I gave him 2 peanuts for 1 penny.
>
> Now I have 2 peanuts and 1 penny.

Then ask each child the following questions. Encourage the children to tell the story as a unit.

1  What did you have in the beginning?

2  Who did you trade with?

3  What did you trade?

4  What do you have now?

**7. Drawing Pictures of the Trading**

Get the children to illustrate their own individual trading experience as follows:

1  Draw a picture of what you had in the beginning. If you had two pennies in the beginning, you can draw two circles like this:

2  If you had four peanuts in the beginning, you can draw them like this:

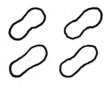

3  Now draw what you have left.

Help the children draw their pictures so that they represent what they had in the beginning and what they have left now. Talk about the fact that their pictures mean the same as the actual pennies and peanuts. This exercise and others like it will help the children to realize that what is real can be represented and that they can use the representations to mean the same as the real objects.

Listed below are variations to this lesson that you might like to try.

**VARIATIONS**

1 Use different items: beads, crayons, balloons, candies, etc.

2 Vary the number of items in each envelope; for example, put three pennies in one envelope and nine peanuts in another to give a ratio of three to one.

3 Give everyone the same; for example, five pennies and five peanuts in each envelope and encourage the children to trade.

# Lesson B-5   A Problem-Solving Situation —
# Comparing with Cubes

**PURPOSES**

- To develop story problems by building and comparing with cubes or blocks of the same size.

- To develop language skills: *longest, shortest, tallest, smallest.*

**MATERIALS NEEDED**

- Cubes or blocks (Unifix Cubes work well) of various colors.

- Various sticks, poles, etc. of arbitrary lengths that children can measure with.

**DIRECTIONS**

**1. Introduction**

Give the children as many cubes as they can reasonably count and ask them to build whatever they like. If they are slow getting started, give them some ideas: towers, trains, railroad tracks, etc.

**2. Discussion**

When everyone is finished, talk about what they made:

*A train.*     1   What did you make?

*Johnny did.*  2   Who else made a train?

*Yes.*         3   Sammy, did you make a train?

**3. Story Problem**

*Note: Do not develop story problems comparing trains when one is very much longer than the other. There should be some difference in length, but not an obvious one.*

Generate a story problem from the children's answers. For example:

Johnny and Sammy both made trains.

Whose train is the longest?

**4. Major Problem-Solving Approach**

Ask the children the following questions:

*Trains.*

1 What is the story about?

*Sammy and Johnny.*

2 Who made the trains?

*Which train is the longest?*

3 What do we want to find out?

4 How can we find out which train is the longest? (The children may come up with various ideas such as counting the number of blocks used in each train, using arbitrary measures like their hands, sticks, etc.) If they have not thought of just putting the two trains side by side and comparing, ask them:

*Ask them to stand back to back.*

5 Is there another way of finding out which train is the longest without counting or measuring? Give the children hints; for example: If we wanted to find out who was the tallest, Johnny or Sammy, what would we do?

*Yes.*

6 Could we find out whose train is the longest by putting them side by side?

Try to elicit as many ways as possible from the children as to how they can find out whose train is the longest. When a number of possibilities have been suggested, ask each child:

*By looking at them; by measuring; by comparing, etc.*

7 How did you find out which train was the longest?

Continue this procedure of generating story problems about the other things the children make. Use the questions in the major problem-solving approach if the children have difficulty in solving the story problems. Listed below are types of story problems that could be generated from the activity.

**STORY PROBLEMS**

1 Kelly and Sandra have both made towers. Whose tower is the tallest/ smallest?

2 Lisa and Nick made railroad tracks. Whose railroad tracks are the longest/ shortest?

3 Anna and Mike and Jordan made snakes. Whose snake is the longest/ shortest?

# Lesson B-6    Making Trains

PURPOSES

- To develop story problem understandings by making trains.

- To expand the initial steps of the major problem-solving approach to include asking the children to tell how they will solve the story problem.

MATERIALS NEEDED

- Cut out rectangles of paper about 4″ × 8″ to use as carriages.

- Tape and crayons.

DIRECTIONS

1. Introduction

Give each child a rectangle of paper and ask what shape it is. Tell them that they can make trains with the rectangles by sticking them together with some tape. Every rectangle is a carriage or train car, and the tape will join the carriages together. First they have to draw windows on a rectangle to make it a carriage. Then they can have another rectangle to make another carriage. Let the children draw people, doors, and designs on their carriages. Show them how to stick the tape on, and help them with their drawings if necessary.

2. Discussion

When everyone has finished, ask the children the following questions:

1  How many carriages do you have on your train?

2  How many windows did you put in your carriages?

3  Did you put doors or people in your carriages?

3. Story Problem

Generate a story problem from the children's responses.

Barbara has 7 carriages in her train.

Tim has 5 carriages in his train.

How many more carriages does Barbara have?

**4. Major Problem-Solving Approach**

*Trains, carriages.*

*How many more carriages does Barbara have?*

*Barbara has 7 carriages, and Tim has 5 carriages.*

**7**

**5**

*By taking away the number of carriages Tim has from the number of carriages Barbara has; by taking 5 from 7; by matching the trains and counting the number of carriages that are left.*

Discuss the problem with the children by asking them the following questions:

1 What is the story problem about?

2 What do we have to find out?

3 What do you need to know to find out how many more carriages Barbara has?

4 If the previous question is too difficult for the children, try:

How many carriages does Barbara have?

How many carriages does Tim have?

5 How will we find out how many more carriages Barbara has?

The emphasis of this lesson is on building the language and focusing on the concepts necessary to solve story problems. At this stage it is not necessary to solve the story problems, but you may do so if you wish.

Listed below are several types of story problems that you could generate from this activity. Follow a similar procedure when talking through the story problems with the children.

**TYPES OF STORY PROBLEMS**

1 Phil has 7 carriages in his train. Martin has 8 carriages. Who has more carriages?

2 Jill and Peter both made trains. Whose train is the longest?

3 Amy and Sally both made trains. Whose train is the shortest?

4 Ed has 6 carriages in his train. Alice has 4 carriages in her train. If they join their trains, how many carriages will they have altogether?

# Lesson B-7 Making Greeting Cards

**PURPOSES**
- To develop story problems by making greeting cards.

- To talk about the activity (how many cards the children made, for whom, etc.).

- To solve story problems based on the activity by using the initial steps of the major problem-solving approach.

**MATERIALS NEEDED**
- Duplicated copies of the greeting cards. (See the picture page at the end of the lesson.)

- Crayons and colored pencils for coloring.

- Aluminum foil, transparent colored paper, wool, etc., for decorating.

- Glue, paste, and sticks for pasting.

- Envelopes.

**DIRECTIONS**

**1. Making the Cards**

Make copies of the cards on the following page (see Cards for Lesson B-7) and cut them out. Let the children have access to all the materials and let them begin. Make a card yourself if necessary to give them an idea. Write greetings on the blackboard for those children who can copy them and help the others to write their greetings. Encourage the children to make a lot of cards and to decorate them.

**2. Discussion**

When everyone has completed several cards, tell them that it is time to put the cards into envelopes. Talk about the cards they made.

1  How many cards did you make?

2  Who are you going to send them to?

**3. Story Problem**

Develop a story problem based on what the children have done; for example:

Brian made 3 cards: 1 for his mother, 1 for his father, and 1 for the teacher. How many envelopes will Brian need?

If the children know immediately that the answer is three envelopes, tell them that they are right. However, whether they know the answer or not, repeat the story again and ask them the following questions:

*Brian's cards.*

1 What is the story about?

*3 cards.*

2 How many cards did Brian make?

*Brian's mother, father, and teacher.*

3 Who were they for?

*How many envelopes does Brian need for his cards?*

4 What do we want to find out in the story?

*Brian made 3 cards.*

5 What do we need to know to find out how many envelopes Brian needs?

*By matching; by counting.*

6 How will we find out how many envelopes Brian needs?

7 Count together or match to find out how many envelopes Brian needs.

*Brian needs 3 envelopes.*

8 How many envelopes does Brian need?

Give Brian three envelopes.

The above questions help the children to focus on the essential details of the story problem. These questions or steps are very useful when a child does not immediately understand a problem. Even if the children know the answer, it is very important to develop the language necessary for solving problems; asking these questions now can help the children later when they are confronted with a problem that they cannot solve. After repeated exposure, they will slowly learn to ask these questions for themselves.

Generate similar story problems from the activity and solve them using the questions in the major problem-solving approach. (See Chapter 1 to review the use of this major problem-solving approach.)

Listed below are story problems that could be generated from the activity.

**STORY PROBLEMS**

1 Anne made only 1 card. Jack made 2. How many cards did they make altogether?

2 Danny made 4 cards. I gave him 2 envelopes. How many more envelopes does he need?

3 Sarah made 3 cards. Ginny made 4. Who made more cards?

4 Alice made 5 cards. Two are for her Mom and the rest are for her Dad. How many cards did Alice make for her Dad?

5 I want to mail my card. A stamp costs 20¢. I have only 10¢. How much more money do I need?

Name _____

Happy _____

To: _____
From: _____

Happy _____

To: _____
From: _____

Happy _____

To: _____
From: _____

Happy _____

To: _____
From: _____

# Lesson B-8　Children Compose Story Problems from Nature

PURPOSES
- To gather items from nature (worms, stones, etc.).
- To devise story problems about the items gathered.

MATERIALS NEEDED
- Five or six shovels.
- Portion of a garden, or other location, for digging.
- Jar with punctured lid in which to put worms, insects, etc.
- Magnifying glass.

DIRECTIONS

**1. Digging**　Work with a group of five children. Let them dig away and encourage them to save what they find in the earth. Get them to put the worms, insects, and other things that they find in the jar. They can look at the worms through a magnifying glass.

**2. Discussion**　Ask the children the following questions:

1　What did you find?

2　How many worms/stones/etc. did you find? (If necessary, help the children count their findings.)

3　What do they look like?

4　What color are they?

*They crawl about.*　5　How do worms move about?

*In the ground.*　6　Where do worms live?

7　What do worms eat?

*Birds.*　8　Who eats worms?

**3. Children's Story Problems**

Tell the children a story problem to give them the idea, such as:

Erin found 2 worms.

Jeremy found 3 worms.

Who found more worms?

Then ask the children: Can anyone else tell a story problem about our digging? Help the children if necessary. For example:

*2 stones.*

1 Michelle, what did you find?

*Andy found 5 stones.*

2 Did anyone else find stones?

3 Tell me a story problem about the stones you and Andy found.

Michelle found 2 stones.

Andy found 5 stones.

How many stones were found in all?

Repeat the children's story problems and solve them using the materials they found. If the children have any difficulty in solving the problems, use the steps in the major problem-solving approach (see Chapter 1 for details) to help them work through the "tough spots."

**VARIATIONS**

1 Children could go to the park and collect flowers, weeds, acorns, pine-cones, etc. When they return, they should make up story problems about what they found.

2 Children could make up story problems about a cooking activity.

# Lesson B-9   Nature Study with Pictures

PURPOSES
- To solve story problems using nature pictures.
- To talk about each picture with the children.
- To solve the story problems by using the steps from the major problem-solving approach.

MATERIALS NEEDED
- Copy of the pictures for each child. (See Pictures for Lesson B-9 at the end of the lesson.)
- Crayons.

DIRECTIONS

**1. Introduction**

Give each child a copy of the pictures and ask the children to look at the first picture at the top of the page. Discuss the picture with the children.

*Bees.*

1  What do you see in the picture?

*Yes, one bee is bigger.*

2  Is one bee different from the rest?

3  The bee that is bigger than the others is a queen bee. She is in charge of the other bees. The other bees are called workers. They collect nectar from the flowers and make honey inside their bodies. Bees are very industrious insects. They store the honey they make in their hives for the long cold winter days.

**2. Story Problem**

Tell the children the following story problem:

> The queen bee scolded 4 bees for being lazy.
>
> She scolded 4 more for eating too much honey.
>
> How many bees did she scold altogether?

**3. Major Problem-Solving Approach**

Discuss the story problem with the children by asking them the following questions:

*Bees.*

1  What is the story problem about?

*How many bees did the queen bee scold altogether?*

2 What do you need to find out?

*The queen bee scolded 4 bees for being lazy and 4 more bees for eating too much honey.*

3 What do you need to know to find out how many bees the queen bee scolded altogether?

*I will count all the bees in the picture.*

4 Look at your picture. How will you find out how many bees the queen bee scolded?

Why?

*Because the picture shows the 4 bees that were scolded for being lazy and the 4 bees that were scolded for eating too much honey.*

5 How many bees do you think were scolded altogether? Were more than four bees scolded?

6 Count to find out how many bees were scolded.

*8 bees were scolded.*

7 How many bees were scolded?

8 Did anyone guess right?

Follow a similar procedure with the following five story problems. Talk about each picture first before solving the story problem. Use the major problem-solving approach if the children have difficulty in solving the problem. Let the children color their pictures at the end of the lesson.

**STORY PROBLEMS**

1 The hedgehog woke up after sleeping all winter long. He was very hungry. The first week he killed and ate 6 newts. The second week he ate 6 more newts. How many newts did the hedgehog eat altogether?

2 Tony ate 2 oranges. He found 4 orange seeds in one orange and 5 in the other. How many orange seeds did he find altogether?

3 A robin had 5 eggs in her nest. She left her nest to look for food. A cuckoo came by and left 1 large egg in the robin's nest. When the robin came back, how many eggs did she find in her nest?

4 Sally opened up 2 sweet peas. She found 5 seeds in one and 6 seeds in the other. How many seeds did she find altogether?

5 An octopus has 8 arms. He uses his arms to catch fish. How many arms do 2 octopi have?

Name _____

Sample:

1.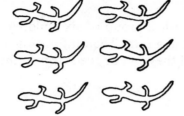

2.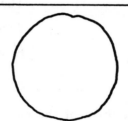

3.

4.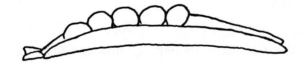

5.

# Lesson B-10   Story Problem Drama

PURPOSES

- To act out story problems in order to help solve them.

- To solve the story problems by using the major problem-solving approach.

DIRECTIONS

**1. Introduction**

Work with a group of six children. Ask them to count how many children are in the group. Then inform them that you are going to tell a story problem and they can be the actors in the story.

**2. Story Problem**

There are 6 children in the group.

3 are sleeping, and the rest are sitting.

How many children are sitting?

**3. Acting out the Story**

Ask three of the children to lie down and pretend that they are sleeping. Then ask the remaining children to sit down.

**4. Major Problem-Solving Approach**

Use the following steps of the major problem-solving approach to talk through the problem with the children.

*Children.*

1  What is the story about?

*Sleeping and sitting.*

2  What are the children doing?

*How many children are sitting?*

3  What do we want to find out?

*There are 6 children; 3 are sleeping, and the rest are sitting.*

4  What do we need to know in order to find out how many children are sitting?

*By counting the children that are sitting; by taking 3 from 6.*

5  How can we find out how many children are sitting?

*Three, four, . . . .*

6  Before we count or take away, how many children do you think are sitting?

Count together the number of children who are sitting.

3 children are sitting.    7   How many children are sitting?

Yes/no.    8   Did you guess right?

Ask the children on the floor to wake up for the next story problem.
Follow a similar procedure with the following story problems. Encourage the children to act out the story problems in order to solve them.

**STORY PROBLEMS**    1   There are 3 girls and 4 boys waiting in line. How many children are waiting in line altogether?

2   8 children were standing. 3 sat down. How many children are still standing?

3   7 children were standing on one leg. 3 got tired and sat down. How many children are still standing on one leg?

4   3 children are clapping their hands. How many hands are clapping?

# Lesson B-11 Vocabulary Development for Story Problems

PURPOSES

- To solve story problems containing two or more different sets, both of which belong to a larger universal set:

| | |
|---|---|
| sparrows and robins | — birds |
| buttercups and daisies | — flowers |
| carrots and cucumbers | — vegetables |
| squirrels and monkeys | — animals |
| swans and ducks | — birds |
| apples, bananas, and oranges | — fruit |

- To solve the story problems by using the major problem-solving approach.

MATERIALS NEEDED

- Pictures for Lesson B-11 (from the end of the lesson) for each child.

- Crayons.

DIRECTIONS

**1. Introduction and Discussion**

Ask the children to look at the first picture at the top of their page. (If too many pictures on the same page are confusing or distracting to the children, cut out each picture, and let the children have them one at a time. Staple the pictures together again at the end of the lesson.) Discuss the first picture with the children by asking them the following questions:

*Some birds and a dog.*

1 What do you see in the picture?

2 What is your favorite bird?

*No, some are smaller than the others.*

3 Do all the birds in your picture look the same?

4 The small birds are called sparrows, and the bigger birds are called robins.

*3*  5 How many sparrows are there?

*3*  6 How many robins are there?

7 What other kinds of birds do you know?

**2. Story Problem**    Tell the children the following story problem:

> Rover chased 3 sparrows and 3 robins.
>
> They flew up into the tree.
>
> How many birds did Rover chase?

**3. Major Problem-
Solving Approach**    Discuss the story problem by asking the children the following questions:

*Birds.*    1    What is the story problem about?

*How many birds did Rover
chase altogether?*    2    What do you need to find out?

*Rover chased 3 sparrows
and 3 robins.*    3    What do you need to know to find out how many birds Rover chased
altogether?

*I will add 3 sparrows to 3
robins; I will count to find
out how many birds there
are in the picture altogether.*    4    How will you find out how many birds Rover chased?

*Five, six, seven . . . .*    5    Guess how many birds you think Rover chased.

*Yes.*        Did he chase more than three birds?

6    Count the birds in the picture to find out how many birds Rover chased.

*Rover chased 6 birds.*    7    How many birds did Rover chase?

8    Did anyone guess correctly?

Follow a similar procedure with the following story problems. Discuss the contents of the picture first with the children and then solve the related story problem together. At the end of the lesson, let the children color their pictures.

**STORY PROBLEMS**    1    The honey bee took nectar from 4 buttercups and 3 daisies, and then she flew back to her hive. How many flowers did the honey bee take nectar from?

2    Jessica chopped up 4 carrots and 3 cucumbers to make the caterpillar salad. How many vegetables did Jessica use?

3 Three squirrels and 2 monkeys are playing in the tree. How many animals are playing in the tree?

4 Two swans, a mother duck, and her 3 baby ducks are swimming in the pond. How many birds are swimming in the pond altogether?

5 Paul made a fruit salad for a party. He used 3 apples, 3 bananas, and 3 oranges. How many pieces of fruit did Paul use?

Name_____

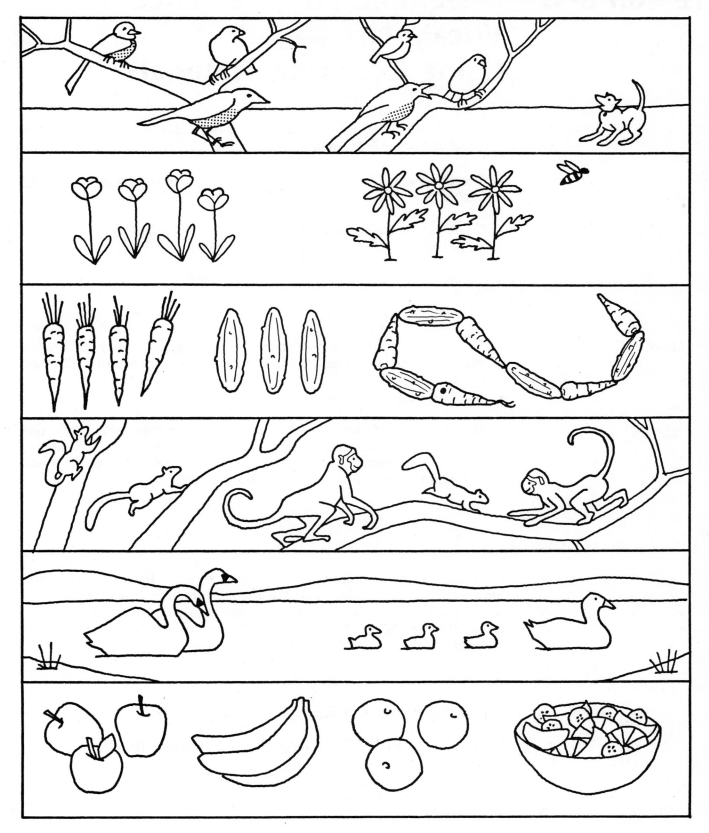

# Lesson B-12 Developing Mathematical Vocabulary — Using Concrete Materials

**PURPOSES**

- To develop story problems containing the following mathematical vocabulary: *more, least, equal.*

- For the children to manipulate concrete materials to help solve the story problems.

- To follow the steps of the major problem-solving approach to solve the story problems.

- To make rubbings with the materials at the end of the lesson.

**MATERIALS NEEDED**

- Leaves, coins, and keys or similar items. (These items were chosen because the children can make rubbings with them at the end of the lesson.)

- Crayons, pencils, and paper.

- Sample of a leaf rubbing, a key rubbing, and a coin rubbing. (Simple rubbings can be made by placing a sheet of paper over a leaf and rubbing hard with a crayon. The pattern of the leaf will come through. Coin rubbings turn out well when a thick-leaded pencil is used.)

**DIRECTIONS**

**1. Introduction**

Show the children samples of a leaf rubbing, a coin rubbing, and a key rubbing. Tell them that they can make rubbings too, but first they are going to solve some story problems. Ask who wants to make a leaf rubbing first. Choose two children and give one five leaves and the other four leaves. Ask each child to count how many leaves he or she has.

**2. Story Problem**

Tell the children the following story problem:

Amy and Derek are going to make leaf rubbings.

Amy has 5 leaves. Derek has 4 leaves.

Who has *more* leaves?

**3. Major Problem-Solving Approach**

*Leaves.*

*Who has more leaves.*

*Amy has five leaves, and Derek has four leaves.*

*By looking to see who has the most; by matching; by counting.*

Discuss the story problem with the children by asking them the following questions:

1 What is the story problem about?

2 What do you need to find out?

3 What do you need to know to find out who has more leaves?

4 How will you find out who has more leaves?

5 Compare the number of leaves each child has by matching. Ask Amy to put one of her leaves on the table. Ask Derek to put one of his leaves below Amy's leaf. Repeat this process until all the leaves have been matched one to one and Derek has no more leaves left.

Amy     🍁    🍃    🍂    🍃    🍁

Derek     🍃    🍂    🍁    🍃

*Amy has more leaves.*

6 Derek has no more leaves left, but Amy has one leaf left. Who has more leaves?

*One more leaf.*

7 How many more leaves does Derek need so that both he and Amy have an *equal* amount?

Follow a similar procedure with the story problems listed below. Use the major problem-solving approach if the children have difficulty in solving the story problems.

**STORY PROBLEMS**

1 Give Tony 5 coins and Alice 7 coins to make coin rubbings:

Tony and Alice are going to make coin rubbings.

Tony has 5 coins. Alice has 7 coins.

Who has *more* coins?

How many more coins does Tony need so that he and Alice have an *equal* amount?

2 Give Sue 3 keys, Joe 2 keys, and Katie 5 keys to make key rubbings:

Sue, Joe, and Katie are going to make key rubbings.

Sue has 3 keys, Joe has 2 keys, and Katie has 5 keys.

Who has the *least* keys?

3  Give Andy 5 crayons, Mary 3 crayons, and Derek 4 crayons to make their rubbings with.

Andy has 5 crayons.

Mary has 3 crayons.

Derek has 4 crayons.

Who has the *least* crayons?

**RUBBINGS**  At the end of the lesson, give each child a sheet of paper and some pencils. Also give some crayons to those children who did not receive any during the lesson. Show the children how to make a rubbing. Taping the paper to their desks will prevent it from sliding. Let them swap their materials to make different kinds of rubbings. Ask them to look for other materials in the classroom that they could also make rubbings of.

# Lesson B-13 Devising Neighborhood Walk Story Problems

PURPOSES

- To encourage the children to talk about where they went, what they saw, and what they did.

- To develop stories about what happened on the walk.

- To help the children to ask questions so that the stories become story problems.

MATERIALS NEEDED

- Make a copy of the Neighborhood Walk Chart for each child. (See Chart for Lesson B-13 at the end of the lesson.)

- Pencils and crayons.

DIRECTIONS

**1. Discussion**

Give each child a copy of the Chart and talk about it:

*A bicycle, a motorcycle, a truck, a van, a bus, and a store.*

1  What pictures do you see on the chart?

2  Where do you see bicycles/motorcycles/trucks/vans/buses/stores?

**2. Neighborhood Walk**

Take the children on a walk around your locality. Encourage them to look for what they can see on their charts and to mark an X every time they see one of the items listed.

**3. Discussion after the Walk**

Talk with the children about where they went, what they did, and what they saw. Tell the children to look at their charts and ask them:

1  How many bicycles did you see? (Count the X's under the bicycle picture on your chart. If you need help, ask me please.)

2  How many motorcycles did you see?

3  How many trucks did you see?

4  How many vans did you see?

5  How many stores did you see?

6  How many buses did you see?

**4. Story**  Using the information given in the discussion, tell the children a story. For example:

Joe saw two motorcycles, and Sandy saw five motorcycles.

I can make a story problem by asking the question: Who saw more motorcycles? or How many more motorcycles did Sandy see than Joe?

**5. Children Complete the Story**  Tell the children another story based on their graphs. For example:

John saw 4 bicycles, and Erin saw 5 bicycles.

Can anyone turn the story into a story problem?

Encourage the children to think up questions for the story and prompt them if necessary. Suggest your own questions if it becomes too difficult for them.

Repeat the story with the children's questions (see below) and solve the story problems using their charts. Use the major problem-solving approach (see Chapter 1 for details) if the children have difficulty in solving their story problems.

**STORY PROBLEMS**  1  John saw 4 bicycles, and Erin saw 5 bicycles. Who saw more bicycles?

2  John saw 4 bicycles, and Erin saw 5 bicycles. Did John see more bicycles than Erin?

3  John saw 4 bicycles, and Erin saw 5 bicycles. Did Erin see more bicycles than John?

4  John saw 4 bicycles, and Erin saw 5 bicycles. How many more bicycles did Erin see than John?

Name _____

| | |
|---|---|
| store | |
| bus | |
| van | |
| truck | |
| motorcycle | |
| bicycle | |

# Lesson B-14   Solving Story Problems by Drawing Pictures

PURPOSES

- To show the children how to draw pictures of each story problem by connecting dotted lines.

- To help the children to use their picture to solve the story problems.

- To discuss with the children how their picture helps them to solve the story problems.

- To follow the steps of the major problem-solving approach.

MATERIALS NEEDED

- Copy of the dotted line pictures for each child. (See Pictures for Lesson B-14 at the end of the lesson.)

- Pencils.

DIRECTIONS

1. Introduction

Give each child a copy of the pictures and explain to the children that they can draw a picture of each story problem by connecting the dots with a pencil.

2. Story Problem

Tell the children the following story problem:

> Lynn bought 5 balloons at the store.
>
> On her way home she burst 2 balloons.
>
> How many balloons does Lynn have left?

3. Children Draw the Story Problem

Ask the children to look at the top of their page.

*Dots.*

1   What do you see?

*A picture of balloons.*

2   If you draw a line through all the dots, what picture will you get?

3   Children draw the balloons.

| | |
|---|---|
| *5* | 4  How many balloons did you draw altogether? |
| *5* | 5  How many balloons did Lynn buy at the store? |

### 4. Major Problem-Solving Approach

Repeat the story problem to the children and ask them the following questions:

*Balloons.*

1  What is the story problem about?

*How many balloons does Lynn have left?*

2  What do you need to find out?

*Lynn had 5 balloons, and and she burst 2 of them.*

3  What do you need to know to find out how many balloons Lynn has left?

*I drew 5 balloons.*

4  Look at your picture. How many balloons did you draw?

*I will take 2 balloons away from the 5 balloons Lynn had in the beginning.*

How will you find out how many balloons Lynn has left?

*Because Lynn burst 2 of her balloons.*

Why?

*Yes, maybe 3 or 4 balloons.*

5  How many balloons do you think Lynn has left? Does she have less than five balloons?

*3*

6  Ask the children to cover two balloons with their hand and count to see how many balloons are left.

*Lynn has 3 balloons left.*

7  How many balloons does Lynn have left? Get the children to give the full answer sentence.

8  Did anyone guess right?

Follow a similar procedure with the following three story problems. First tell the children the story problem and then have them draw the picture by connecting all the dots. Encourage them to use their pictures to help them to solve the story problem.

### STORY PROBLEMS

1  Jim had 5 toy boats. He sailed his boats down the river, but 1 boat sank. How many boats does Jim have left?

2  Jenny has 4 toy cars. Andy has 1 more than Jenny. How many toy cars does Andy have?

3  Sally, Lisa, and Barry are sending their rockets to outer space. They have 3 rockets each. How many rockets are going to outer space altogether?

Name _____

 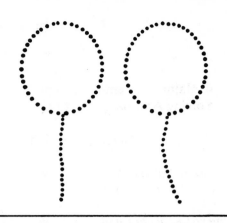

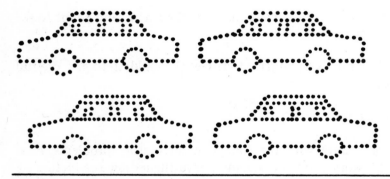 

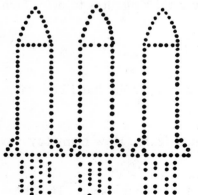  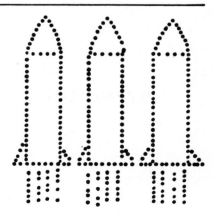

# Lesson B-15 Solving Story Problems by Drawing Pictures

**PURPOSES**

- To show the children how to draw a picture about a story problem.

- To help children to use their picture to solve the story problem.

- To discuss with the children how their picture helps them to solve the story problem.

- To follow the steps of the major problem-solving approach to help solve the story problems.

**DIRECTIONS**

**1. Story Problem**

Tell the children the following story problem:

> Sally played marbles with her brother Tom.
>
> She had 3 marbles in the beginning, and she won 2 more.
>
> How many marbles does Sally have now?

**2. Children Draw a Picture of the Story Problem**

Tell the children to draw three circles for the marbles Sally had in the beginning. Then get them to draw two more circles for the marbles she won from her brother Tom.

**3. Major Problem-Solving Approach**

Repeat the story problem to the children and ask them the following questions:

*Marbles.*

1  What is the story problem about?

*How many marbles does Sally have now?*

2  What do you need to find out?

*Sally had 3 marbles, and she won 2 from her brother Tom.*

3  What do you need to know to find out how many marbles Sally has now?

*I will count the number of marbles I have drawn altogether.*

4  Look at your picture. How will you find out how many marbles Sally has now?

*Because I drew the 3 marbles Sally had in the beginning and the 2 she won from her brother Tom.*

Why?

*Four, five, six marbles.*

5 How many marbles do you think Sally has now?

6 Count to find out how many marbles Sally has.

*Sally has 5 marbles.*

7 How many marbles does Sally have?

8 Did anyone guess right?

Follow a similar procedure with the following three word problems. First tell the children each story problem and then help them to draw a corresponding picture. Encourage them to use their pictures to help solve the story problem.

**STORY PROBLEMS**

1 Paul bought 6 eggs at the store. On the way home he fell off his bike and broke 2 of the eggs. How many eggs did Paul bring home?

2 Katie had 5 pennies. Her tooth fell out, and the Tooth Fairy gave her 5 more pennies. How many pennies does Katie have now?

3 Tom climbed up the apple tree in his back yard and picked 5 juicy red apples. He ate 1 when he was up in the tree. How many apples does Tom have left?

# Lesson B-16 Reviewing the Major Problem-Solving Approach — Story Problems with Pictures

**PURPOSES**
- To review the steps of the major problem-solving approach.
- To solve story problems based on pictures.
- To use the pictures as an aid in solving the story problems.

**MATERIALS NEEDED**
- A copy of the pictures for each child. (See Pictures for Lesson B-16 at the end of the lesson.)

**DIRECTIONS**

**1. Discussion**

Ask the children to look at the picture on the top of their page and ask them the following questions:

*Dimes.*

1  What do you see in the picture?

*2 groups.*

2  How many groups of dimes do you see?

*3*

3  How many dimes are in each group?

**2. Story Problem**

Ask the children to look at the picture again and tell them the following story problem:

> Rebecca had 3 dimes.
>
> Her father gave her 3 more for cleaning up the yard.
>
> How many dimes does Rebecca have now?

**3. Major Problem-Solving Approach**

Discuss the story problem with the children by asking them the following questions:

*Dimes.*

1  What is the story problem about?

*How many dimes does Rebecca have now?*

2  What do you need to find out?

*Rebecca had 3 dimes, and her father gave her 3 more.*

3  What do you need to know to find out how many dimes Rebecca has now?

*I will count to see how many dimes are in the picture.*

4  Look at your picture. How will you find out how many dimes Rebecca has now?

Why?

*Because the picture shows the 3 dimes Rebecca had in the beginning and the 3 dimes her father gave her.*

*Yes, she has about five, six, seven dimes.*

5  How many dimes do you think Rebecca has now? Does Rebecca have more than three dimes now?

6  Count to find out how many dimes Rebecca has now.

*Rebecca has 6 dimes now.*

7  How many dimes does Rebecca have now?

8  Did anyone guess right?

Follow a similar procedure with the following five story problems. Use the major problem-solving approach if the children have difficulty in solving the story problems. Get the children to use their pictures to solve the story problems, and let them color their pictures at the end of the lesson.

**STORY PROBLEMS**

1  Mary likes to climb trees. She climbed 2 trees in her front garden and 3 trees in her back garden. How many trees did Mary climb altogether?

2  Anne picked 4 roses. She put 1 in her hair and the rest in a jar of water. The rose in her hair died because it needed water. How many roses does Anne have left?

3  John loves to play baseball. He had 5 baseballs, and at Christmas he got 3 more baseballs. How many baseballs does John have now?

4  Dave climbed up an orange tree and picked 5 oranges. He squeezed 2 to make orange juice. How many oranges does Dave have left?

5  Sue got 10 storybooks for her birthday. She read 7 of them all by herself, and her father read the rest to her. How many storybooks did Sue's father read to her?

Name_____

**Sample**

1.

2.

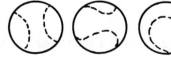    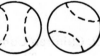

3.

4.

5.

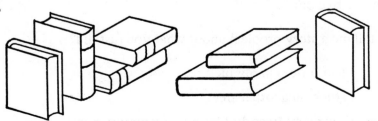 

# Lesson B-17    Children Compose Story Problems

PURPOSES

- To make a picture of a forest.

- For the children to compose their own story problems based on the activity.

MATERIALS NEEDED

- Cut-out trees. (Tree Pictures for Lesson B-17 are located at the end of the lesson.)

- Paper, paste, and crayons.

DIRECTIONS

1. Introduction

Duplicate the trees. (See Pictures for Lesson B-17 on the following page and cut them out.) Have each child color a number of trees and then paste them onto a blank sheet of paper to make a forest. Let the children paste on as many trees as they like and encourage them to overlap the trees. When everyone has finished, ask each child:

How many trees are there in your forest?

2. Children Compose Their Own Story Problems

First tell the children a story problem to give them the idea. For example:

Anne has 5 trees in her picture.

Jack has 7 trees in his.

How many more trees does Jack have?

Can anyone else tell a story problem about their picture? Help the children if necessary. For example, you could encourage a child as follows:

*Six trees.*  1  How many trees are in your picture?

2  Stick another tree on.

3  Can you tell me a story problem about what you just did?

I had 6 trees in my picture.

I stuck on another tree.

How many trees do I have in my picture now?

Repeat the children's story problems and solve them using their pictures. If the children have any difficulty in solving their story problems, use the major problem-solving approach to help them work through the "tough spots." (The steps to this approach are outlined in Chapter 1.)

**VARIATIONS**

1 Give each child a picture of a tree trunk with branches and cut-out leaves to stick on their trees. Encourage them to compose a story about how many leaves are on their trees, whose tree has the most leaves, etc.

2 Children could make up story problems based on the different types of trees in a forest.

Name_____

# Chapter 3

# GRADE 1
# PROBLEM-SOLVING
# LESSONS
## (LEVEL I )

By the time children reach first grade, they are ready to deal with story and word problems, as long as the problems they are asked to solve are meaningful and interesting to them. The lessons for this level are designed to appeal to and meet the needs of first-grade children. At the same time they are organized to develop children's skills for solving more difficult problems. In order to accomplish these goals, the major problem-solving approach, as outlined in Chapter 1, is introduced in the initial lessons and then further developed throughout.

The supporting techniques for this level include a wide range of activities (drawing, nature study, composing our own story problems, developing language and mathematical vocabulary, etc.), thereby integrating math with many other areas of the curriculum. These supporting techniques are introduced and developed in specific lessons.

Many of the lessons are based on concrete materials, physical activities, or pictures of situations, with a gradual introduction to more formal problem solving. However, manipulatives and/or simple pictures and diagrams may be used with any problem in the sequence in order to enhance student understanding. With the solid background of these problem-solving lessons, the students will gain the ability to solve more difficult and abstract problems.

Each lesson begins with plans for the teacher, including suggested questions and responses for a sample problem; then, when appropriate, a copy of the student page follows immediately. This arrangement provides the teacher with immediate access to Purposes, Materials, Directions, and Answers for the lesson as well as a copy of the student page. Any student problem pages or supplemental problem-solving aids (such as pictures and charts) in the chapter may be duplicated in quantities needed for the teacher's own classroom use.

Although the lessons have been designed primarily to develop problem-solving skills, they also provide computation practice appropriate for children working at the first-grade level. Problems 1 and 2 for each lesson provide easy computations; Problems 3, 4, and 5 are more difficult. The bonus problem might be completed only by the more advanced students. In addition, students who are not able to accomplish the problems at this level may work with easier problems, from the Beginners Chapter (Level B), and students who are able to do advanced work could be assigned the problems from Grade 2 (Level L ).

# Lesson I-1  Introducing the Major Problem-Solving Approach

PURPOSE

- To introduce the children to the initial steps of the major problem-solving approach by:

  1 Finding the main idea in the problem.

  2 Determining what is needed.

  3 Determining the important facts in the problem.

DIRECTIONS

**1. Sample Problem**

Read the following story problem slowly with the children:

> Joan bought a box of 6 pencils.
>
> She lost 2 pencils.
>
> How many does she have left?

**2. Major Problem-Solving Approach**

Discuss the story problem with the children by asking them the following questions:

*Pencils.*

1 What is the story problem about?

*How many pencils does Joan have?*

2 What is the question? What do you want to find out to solve the story problem?

*Joan had 6 pencils, and she lost 2 of them.*

3 What do you need to know to solve the story problem? What do you need to know to find out how many pencils Joan has now?

Follow a similar procedure with the story problems for Lesson I-1 on the student page. It may be helpful to use manipulatives or draw simple pictures of the problem situations. It is not necessary for the children to solve the problems; but if they want to, it is permissible. Be certain to discuss each story problem with the children.

OPTIONAL ANSWERS
(For Student Problems)

*Sample*  Joan has 4 pencils left.

1 Sue has 6 apples altogether.

2 Tom has 6 chocolate chip cookies left.

3   There are 5 roses left on the rosebush.

4   Barbara and John have 10 crayons altogether.

5   The monkey ate 6 bananas altogether.

*Bonus*   3 ants are left in the garbage can.

**LESSON I-1**

**SAMPLE PROBLEM**

Joan bought a box of 6 pencils. She

lost 2 pencils. How many pencils

does she have left?

---

| | |
|---|---|
| 1　Sue climbed a [tree] and picked 4 [apple] . She climbed another [tree] and picked 2 [apple] . How many apples does Sue have altogether? | 2　Tom made 8 chocolate chip [cookies] . He ate 2 [cookies] while they were still hot. How many chocolate chip cookies does Tom have left? |
| 3　There were 7 [rose] on the [bush] . Mary picked 2. How many roses are left? | 4　Barbara has 4 [crayon] . John has 6 [crayon] . How many crayons do they have altogether? |
| 5　A [monkey] at the zoo ate 3 [banana] on Monday, 1 [banana] on Tuesday, and 2 [banana] on Wednesday. How many bananas did the monkey eat altogether? | *Bonus*　Tim counted 8 [ants] in the [trash can] . He squashed 2 [ants] and put 3 other [ants] in his pocket. How many ants are left in the garbage can? |

# Lesson 1-2 Using the Major Problem-Solving Approach

PURPOSE

- To review and expand the initial steps of the major problem-solving approach by:

    1 Finding the main idea in the story problem.

    2 Determining what is wanted, i.e., the question.

    3 Determining the important facts in the story problem.

    4 Stating how to solve the story problem.*

    5 Writing a number sentence for the story problem.*

    6 Computing the answer.*

    7 Stating the answer in a sentence.*

DIRECTIONS

**1. Sample Problem**

Read the following story problem slowly to the children:

> Beth had 7 candy canes.
>
> She ate 2 candy canes.
>
> How many does she have left?

**2. Major Problem-Solving Approach**

*Note: At this stage it is important that the children use each step when working through problems with you. When working on their own, they may eliminate steps, but they should know what the steps are so that they can refer back if they have any difficulty.*

*Candy canes.*

Lead the children to a solution of the problem by using the following types of questions:

1 What is the story problem about?

*How many candy canes does Beth have left?*

2 What is the question? What do you want to find out to solve the story problem?

---

*Steps 4 through 7 are being introduced here for the first time.

*Beth had 7 candy canes, and she ate 2 of them.*

3   What do you need to know to solve the story problem? What do you need to know to find out how many candy canes Beth has left?

*I will take the number of candy canes Beth ate away from the number of candy canes Beth had in the beginning.*

4   How will you solve the story problem? How will you find out how many candy canes Beth has left?

*Subtract.*

What operation will you use? Will you add or subtract?

A picture of the situation might be helpful:

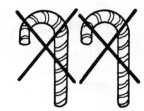

5   Write a number sentence for this problem on the blackboard: (7 − 2 = _____) Have the children copy the number sentence on their worksheets.

6   Subtract using your number sentence. What is your answer?

*Beth has 5 candy canes left.*

7   Give your answer in a sentence.

Follow a similar procedure with the story problems for Lesson 1-2 on the following page. You may wish to do one or two problems together to give the children practice at using the steps and then just read the remaining story problems with the children, letting them do the last few on their own. You may wish to allow the students to use manipulatives and/or you may draw pictures of the problem situations. Discuss each problem with the children as they finish it.

**ANSWERS**
**(For Student Problems)**

1   Joe has 7 goldfish now.

2   3 balloons are left.

3   Ray has 8 toy cars now.

4   Peter's mother has 9 rabbits altogether.

5   7 ducks are swimming in the pond now.

*Bonus*   Jan used 7 leaves in her picture.

Name_____

**SAMPLE PROBLEM**

Beth had 7 [candy cane] . She ate 2

[candy cane] . How many candy canes does Beth have left?

---

1  Joe had 4 [goldfish] . He went

to the [PET STORE] and bought 3

more. How many goldfish does

Joe have now?

---

2  Anne had 8 [balloon] . 5 [balloon] burst. How

many balloons are left?

---

3  Ray had 5 toy [car] . He

got 3 more for his birthday. How

many toy cars does he have now?

(Draw the toy cars.)

---

4  Peter's mother raises

[rabbit] . She has 7 white [rabbit]

and 2 brown [rabbit] . How many

rabbits does she have altogether? (Use your

crayons to draw 7 white rabbits and 2 brown

rabbits.)

---

5  Nine [duck] were swimming in

a [pond] . Two flew

away. How many ducks are

swimming in the pond now?

---

*Bonus*  Jan collected 15 [leaf] .

She painted 3 [leaf] blue

and 4 [leaf] red and

made a [picture] with the

painted leaves. How many

leaves did Jan use in her

picture?

# Lesson I-3    Expanding the Major Problem-Solving Approach

PURPOSE

- To review and expand the steps of the major problem-solving approach by:

    1   Finding the main idea in the story problem.

    2   Determining what is wanted, i.e., the question.

    3   Determining the important facts in the story problem.

    4   Stating how to solve the story problem.

    5   Writing a number sentence for the story problem.

    6   Estimating the answer.*

    7   Computing the answer.

    8   Comparing the answer with the estimation.*

    9   Stating the answer sentence.

## DIRECTIONS

**1. Sample Problem**

Read the following story problem slowly with the children:

> David is learning to ride a horse.
>
> There were 10 horses at the riding school he goes to.
>
> One horse got sick and died.
>
> How many horses are left?

**2. Major Problem-Solving Approach**

Discuss the story problem with the children by asking them the following questions:

*Horses.*

1   What is the story problem about?

*How many horses are left?*

2   What is the question? What do you need to find out to solve the story problem?

*There were 10 horses at the riding school, and 1 died.*

3   What do you need to know to solve the story problem? What do you need to know to find out how many horses are left?

---

*Steps 6 and 8 are being introduced here for the first time. The children may now use all the steps to solve the story problems.

83

*I will take 1 horse away from the number of horses there were in the beginning.*

4 How will you solve the story problem? How will you find out how many horses are left?

5 Write a number sentence for the story problem on the blackboard: $(10 - 1 = \underline{\hspace{1cm}})$ Ask the children to copy the number sentence on their worksheets. (You could also illustrate ten horses and draw an **X** through one.)

6 What do you think your answer will be? Will it be greater or less than 10?

7 Compute the answer together and complete the number sentence.

8 What did you guess your answer would be? Is it the same?

*There are 9 horses left.*  9 Give your answer in a sentence.

Follow a similar procedure with the story problems for Lesson l-3 on the next page. The students may use manipulatives and/or drawings to help them solve the problems. You may wish to do another problem together to give the children practice at using the steps and then just read the remaining story problems with the children and let them solve their own or work in groups. Discuss all the story problems with the children when you have finished.

**ANSWERS
(For Student Problems)**

1 There are 3 football helmets.

2 They saw 10 boats altogether.

3 3 photos did not come out.

4 7 apples are left in the fruit bowl.

5 Anne used 8 slices of bread altogether.

*Bonus* The children made 12 masks altogether.

**SAMPLE PROBLEM**

David is learning to ride a [horse] . There

were 10 horses at the [stable]

he goes to. 1 [horse] got sick and died.

How many horses are left?

---

1   In John's house there are 9 helmets. 6 are

motorcycle [helmet] , and the rest are

football [helmet] . How many football

helmets are there?

---

2   Alison took a walk along the harbor with

her Mom. They saw 4 [boat]

and 6 [sailboat] . How many boats did they

see altogether?

---

3   Rebecca got a new [camera] for her birthday.

She took 8 [photos] , but only 5 came out.

How many photos did not come out?

---

4   Dave's Dad put 10 [apple] in the

[bowl] . Dave was hungry, and he

ate 3. How many apples are left in the

fruit bowl?

---

5   Anne made 4 peanut butter and jelly

[sandwich] . She used 2 [bread] [bread]

for each sandwich. How many slices of

bread did Anne use?

---

*Bonus*   6 children made a scary [mask]

and a funny [mask] each. How

many masks did they make

altogether?

---

# Lesson 1-4　Using Mathematical Vocabulary

**PURPOSES**

- To instruct the children in how to solve story problems using the following mathematical vocabulary: *most, least*.

- To continue the use of the steps of the major problem-solving approach.

**DIRECTIONS**

**1. Sample Problem**

Read the following problem slowly with the children:

> Tammy has 8 kittens.
>
> Tiny has 9 kittens.
>
> Who has the *most* kittens?

**2. Major Problem-Solving Approach**

Discuss the story problem with the children by asking them the following questions:

*Kittens.*

1　What is the story problem about?

*Who has the most kittens?*

2　What do you want to find out to solve the problem? What is the question?

*Tammy has 8 kittens, and Tiny has 9 kittens.*

3　What do you need to know to solve the problem? What do you need to know to find out who has the most kittens?

*I will compare the number of kittens Tammy has to the number of kittens Tiny has and see who has the largest number.*

4　How will you solve the problem? How will you find out who has the most kittens?

*Most.*

5　Which word in the story problem tells you how to solve it?

*Greater.*

Is nine kittens greater or less than eight kittens?

6　Write a number sentence for this problem on the blackboard: ($9 > 8$) Have the children copy the number sentence on their worksheets.

*Tiny has the most kittens.*

7　Give your answer in a sentence.

Follow a similar procedure with the story problems for Lesson 1-4. You may want to do one or two story problems together to give the children practice at using the steps and also to explain the mathematical term *least* to them. Read the rest of the story problems with the children, but let them attempt to solve them on their own. If desired, the students may use manipulatives and/or simple pictures of the problem situations. Discuss all the story problems together when they are finished.

**ANSWERS**
**(For Student Problems)**

1 Katie has the least white mice.

2 Mario's sister has the most records.

3 Lisa painted the least pictures.

4 The least number of books are on the table.

5 Anne has the most marbles.

*Bonus* Robert has the most toy trucks.

**LESSON 1-4**

**SAMPLE PROBLEM**

Tammy has 8  . Tiny has

9  . Who has the *most*

kittens?

---

1  Katie has 7 white [mouse] . Tim has 9

white [mouse] . Who has the *least*

white mice?

2  Mario has 11 [record] . His sister has

12 [record] . Who has the *most* records?

---

3  Laura painted 14 [picture] . Lisa painted

12 [picture] . Who painted the *least*

pictures?

4  There are 16 [book] on the table and 18

[book] on the shelf. Where are the *least*

number of books?

---

5  Anne and her brother are playing marbles.

They have 11 [marbles] altogether. If Anne

has 7 [marbles] , who has the *most* marbles?

*Bonus*  Robert had 4 [truck] , and Joe

had 5 [truck] . Robert's mother

bought him 2 more. Who has the *most*

toy trucks?

---

# Lesson 1-5   Finding Key Words

PURPOSES

- To provide instruction in finding the following key words and phrases and relating them to their appropriate operations:

  "left"        — subtraction
  "in all"      — addition
  "altogether"  — addition

- To further instruct the children in the steps of the major problem-solving approach.

DIRECTIONS

**1. Sample Problem**

Read the following story problem slowly with the children:

Jim cleaned out the junk room.

He found 3 footballs and 4 baseballs.

How many balls did he find *altogether*?

**2. Major Problem-Solving Approach**

Discuss the story problem with the children by asking them the following questions:

*Balls.*

1  What is the story problem about?

*How many balls did Jim find altogether?*

2  What do you want to find out to solve the problem? What is the question?

*Jim found 3 footballs and 4 baseballs.*

3  What do you need to know to solve the story problem? What do you need to know to find out how many balls Jim found?

*Add the number of footballs Jim found to the number of baseballs he found.*

4  How will you solve the story problem? How will you find out how many balls Jim found altogether?

*Altogether.*

5  What operations will you use? Will you add or subtract? Is there any particular word(s) in the story problem that lets you know you must add to find your answer?

*Because the way "altogether" is used here means putting the two sets of balls together.*

Why?

(You may want to show ⬭⬭⬭ + ⬭⬭⬭⬭ = _____ balls.)

6 Write a number sentence for this story problem on the blackboard: (3 + 4 = _____ ) Have the children copy the number sentence on their worksheets.

7 What do you think your answer will be? Will it be greater than or less than 4?

8 Add, using your number sentence. What is your answer?

9 What did you guess your answer would be? Is it the same?

*Jim found 7 balls altogether.*  10 Give your answer in a sentence.

Follow a similar procedure with the story problems for Lesson I-5. You may want to do one or two problems with the children. Then read the remaining story problems with them, but have the children solve them on their own. They may make use of simple drawings and/or manipulatives if helpful. Discuss all the story problems with the children when they have finished.

**ANSWERS**
**(For Student Problems)**

1 4 apples are left.

2 Dave and Karen have 12 toy spacemen altogether.

3 Mary has 8 wasps left.

4 Robin used 14 flowers in the bouquet in all.

5 Jerry used 12 bandages in all.

*Bonus* There are 8 umbrellas in Sara's house altogether.

**SAMPLE PROBLEM**

Jim cleaned out the junk room. He

found 3 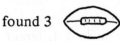 and 4  .

How many balls did he find

*altogether*?

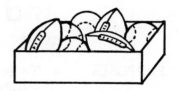

---

| | |
|---|---|
| 1  Jane had 8 🍎 . She used 4 🍎 in a 🥧 . How many apples are *left*? | 2  Dave has 8 toy 👨‍🚀 , and Karen has 4 toy 👨‍🚀 . How many toy spacemen do they have *altogether*? |
| 3  Mary caught 13 🐝 . She let 5 go free. How many wasps does Mary have *left*? | 4  Robin picked 9 🌼 and 5 🌹 to make a 💐 . How many flowers did Robin use in the bouquet *in all*? |
| 5  Jerry fell off the 🪜 and hurt his 🦵 and 🦵 . He used 4 🩹 on his 🦵 and 8 🩹 on his 🦵 . How many bandages did he use *in all*? | *Bonus*  In Sara's 🏠 they are well prepared for the 🌧️ . Her Dad has 3 black ☂️ , and her Mom has 4 ☂️ . Sara has 1 folding ☂️ . How many umbrellas are there in Sara's house *altogether*? |

**91**

# Lesson I-6 Problem Solving and Vocabulary Development

PURPOSES

- To introduce the children to story problems containing two different sets, both of which belong to a larger universal set:

| | |
|---|---|
| wrenches and pliers | — tools |
| piano, violin, saxophone, and flute | — musical instruments |
| moths and butterflies | — insects |
| dogs and pups | — dogs |
| turtles and snakes | — reptiles |
| daisies and buttercups | — flowers |
| sailboats, fishing boats, and motorboats | — boats |

- To review the major problem-solving approach.

DIRECTIONS

**1. Introduction and Discussion**

Talk about tools with the children.

1 A tool is an instrument that people use to help them work.

*Paintbrush, pen, pencil.*

2 What tools do you use?

3 What other tools do you know? How do they help people work?

**2. Sample Problem**

Read the following problem slowly with the children:

Jim has 3 wrenches and 4 pliers in his tool kit.

How many tools does he have altogether?

**3. Major Problem-Solving Approach**

Discuss the story problem with the children by asking them the following questions:

*Tools.*

1 What is the story problem about?

*How many tools does Jim have altogether?*

2 What do you want to find out to solve the story problem? What is the question?

*Jim has 3 wrenches and 4 pliers.*

3 What do you need to know to solve the story problem? What do you need to know to find out how many tools Jim has altogether?

*I will add the number of wrenches Jim has to the number of pliers he has.*

4 How will you solve the story problem? How will you find out how many tools Jim has altogether?

5 Write a number sentence for this problem on the blackboard: (3 + 4 = _____) Have the children copy it on their worksheets.

6 What do you think your answer will be? Will it be greater or less than 4?

7 Compute the answer together and complete the number sentence.

8 What is your answer? What did you guess your answer would be? Is it the same?

*Jim has 7 tools altogether.*

9 Give your answer in a sentence.

Follow a similar procedure with the remaining story problems. Discuss the different sets with the children before they attempt to solve the story problems. Help them to understand the relationship between the sets and a larger universal set. Then let them attempt to solve the story problems on their own. They may use manipulatives and/or simple drawings if helpful. If they have any particular difficulty with one of the story problems, go through the steps of the major problem-solving approach with them. Discuss all story problems with them when you have finished.

ANSWERS
(For Student Problems)

1 Mandy plays 4 musical instruments.

2 Tim saw 8 insects altogether.

3 Dave has 7 dogs altogether.

4 There are 9 reptiles in the picture.

5 Sally and Joel used 12 flowers altogether.

*Bonus* Matt saw 18 boats altogether.

Name_____

**SAMPLE PROBLEM**

Jim has 3 🔧 and 4 🗜️ in his tool kit. How many tools does Jim have altogether?

---

1  Mandy loves music 🎵. She can play the 🎹 , 🎻 , 🎷 , and 🪈 . How many musical instruments can Mandy play?

2  Tim saw 3 🦋 last night and 4 🦋 this morning. How many insects did he see altogether?

---

3  Dave's 🐕 , Tammy, is a mother dog, and she has 3 🐶 . He also has 3 other adult dogs. How many dogs does Dave have altogether?

4  Cathy has a book about reptiles. There is a picture of 4 🐍 and 5 🐢 in her book. How many reptiles are in the picture?

---

5  Sally and Joel are making flower 📿 . Sally made a 📿 of 4 🌼 and 3 🌷 . Joel made a 📿 of 5 🌷 . How many flowers did Sally and Joel use in their necklaces altogether?

*Bonus*  Matt went to the harbor to look at the boats. He counted 4 ⛵ , 5 🚤 , and 9 🛶 . How many boats did Matt see altogether?

---

# Lesson I-7 Problem-Solving with Sea Animal Pictures

**PURPOSES**

- To talk about fish and sea animals.

- To develop story problems about fish and sea animals.

- To develop listening skills.

- To follow the steps of the major problem-solving approach.

**MATERIALS NEEDED**

Make a copy of the pictures for Lesson I-7 (at the end of the lesson) for each child and provide crayons.

**DIRECTIONS**

**1. Introduction and Discussion**

Initiate a discussion about fish by asking the children the following questions:

*In the sea, in rivers, lakes, etc.*

1 Where do fish live?

2 What kinds of fish do you like to eat?

3 What other kinds of fish do you know?

*Smaller fish, plankton.*

4 What do fish eat?

5 Does anyone have any pet fish at home?

6 Did anyone ever go fishing?

**2. Sample Problem**

Ask the children to look at the first picture on their worksheet and tell them the following story problem:

> Codfish like to eat herring.
>
> A codfish was chasing 12 herring.
>
> The codfish caught and ate 2 herring.
>
> How many herring escaped?

## 3. Major Problem-Solving Approach

Discuss the story problem with the children by asking them the following questions:

*Fish, herring.*

1 What is the story problem about?

*How many herring escaped.*

2 What do you need to find out? What is the question?

*A codfish was chasing 12 herring and caught and ate 2 of them.*

3 What do you need to know to solve the story problem? What do you need to know to find out how many herring escaped?

*I will take away the number of herring the codfish ate from the number it was chasing.*

4 How will you solve the story problem? How will you find out how many herring escaped?

*The picture shows the codfish chasing the 12 herring. If I cover 2 herring, I can count to see how many herring are left.*

5 Look at your picture. How can your picture help you to solve the story problem?

6 Write a number sentence for the story problem on the blackboard: $(12 - 2 = \underline{\qquad})$ Have the children copy the number sentence.

7 What do you think your answer will be?

8 Compute the answer together using the picture and complete the number sentence.

9 What did you guess your answer would be? Is it the same?

*10 herring escaped.*

10 Give your answer in a sentence.

Follow a similar procedure with the following story problems. Talk about each picture first and then tell the children the appropriate story problem. Encourage them to use their pictures to solve the story problems. Let them color their pictures at the end of the lesson.

## STORY PROBLEMS

1 The codfish went to visit its friends. A white shark came along and killed 4 codfish and ate them, but 9 codfish escaped. How many codfish were there in the beginning?

2 An octopus has 8 arms to catch small fish with. How many arms do 2 octopi have?

3 A squid has 10 arms to catch small fish with. How many arms do 3 squid have?

4 A starfish has 5 arms. How many arms do 3 starfish have?

*Bonus*  A starfish has 5 arms. An octopus has 8 arms. A squid has 10 arms. How many more arms does a squid have than a starfish?

**ANSWERS**
**(For Student Problems)**

1 There were 13 codfish in the beginning.

2 Two octopi have 16 arms.

3 Three squid have 30 arms.

4 Three starfish have 15 arms.

*Bonus*  A squid has 5 more arms than a starfish.

Name_____

## Sample Problem:

1.

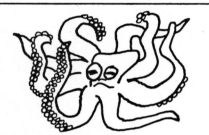

2.

3.

4.

## Bonus Question:

# Lesson 1-8   Oral Presentation of Story Problems Using Concrete Materials

**PURPOSES**

- To develop story problems using materials with which the children can make bookmarks at the end of the lesson.

- To develop listening skills.

- To review the steps of the major problem-solving approach.

**MATERIALS NEEDED**

- Copy the bookmarks at the end of the lesson on construction paper.

- Cut out some of the bookmarks and have the children cut out the rest at the end of the lesson. Also provide scissors, crayons, colored pencils, and felt pens.

**DIRECTIONS**

**1. Introduction**

Begin by telling children that they can make bookmarks for all their books. Talk about bookmarks with them.

1 What is a bookmark?

2 What does a bookmark do?

3 What do people sometimes do when they don't have a bookmark and want to keep their place in a book?

**2. Sample Problem**

Ask one of the children to count how many books he or she has, or ask the child how many bookmarks he or she wants to make. Give the child a smaller number of the cut-out bookmarks and tell the children a story problem based on what you just did. For example:

Pat has 9 books that he wants to decorate bookmarks for.

I gave Pat 5 bookmarks.

How many more bookmarks does Pat want?

**3. Major Problem-Solving Approach**

*Bookmarks.*

*How many more bookmarks does Pat want?*

*Pat wants 9 bookmarks in all, and he has 5.*

*I will use 9 bookmarks and take away 5 to see how many are still needed.*

*I will subtract.*

*Pat wants 4 more bookmarks.*

Solve the story problem using questions from the major problem-solving approach such as:

1  What is the problem about?

2  What question is asked?

3  What facts do you need to know in order to solve the problem?

4  How will you solve the problem?

   Will you add or subtract?

5  Write a number sentence for this story problem on the blackboard: ($9 - 5 = $ _____)

6  Will your answer be more or less than 10?

7  Subtract to find your answer.

8  What is your answer? Is it the same as your guess?

9  Give your answer in a sentence.

Following a similar procedure, give the children the materials they will need to cut out and decorate their bookmarks. Then generate story problems as you give them the materials. Listed below are examples of story problems that you could first act out with the children and then tell them. Substitute the children's names when telling them the story problems. At the end of the lesson, help the children make and decorate their bookmarks and write their names on them.

**TYPES OF STORY PROBLEMS**

1  Jan wants 10 bookmarks. The teacher gave her 5. She will have to cut out the rest herself. How many bookmarks will Jan have to cut out?

2  The teacher gave John 7 colored pencils to decorate his bookmark. The teacher gave Linda 8 colored pencils. Who has the most colored pencils?

3  The teacher gave Jane 10 crayons to decorate her bookmark. The teacher gave Marci 8 crayons. How many crayons do they have altogether?

4  There are 12 children in the group. We have 3 scissors. How many more scissors do we need so that everyone can have one?

5  How many children will have to share scissors if we divide them equally?

*Bonus*  Jim has 6 bookmarks. Sally has 7 bookmarks. Rebecca has 8 bookmarks. How many bookmarks do they have altogether?

Name_____

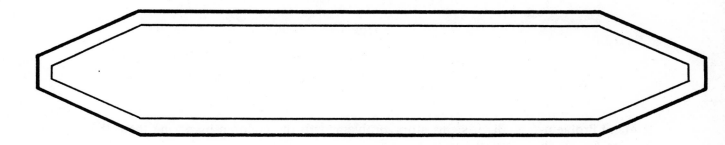

Book
Mark

**101**

# Lesson I-9 Oral Presentation of Problems with Pictures

PURPOSE

- To review the major problem-solving approach by presenting to the children story problems that are accompanied by pictures.

DIRECTIONS

1. Sample Problem

Ask the children to look at their picture of two trains. (See pictures for Lesson I-9 at the end of the lesson). Tell them the following story problem:

> There are 7 carriages in Melissa's train.
>
> Kathryn has 5 carriages in her train.
>
> How many more carriages does Melissa have?

2. Major Problem-Solving Approach

Discuss this story problem with the children by asking them the following questions:

*Carriages.*

1 What is the story problem about?

*How many more carriages does Melissa have?*

2 What is the question? What do you need to find out?

*Trains.*

*2*

*7 and 5*

3 Discuss the picture with the children. What do you see in the picture? How many trains are there? How many carriages are in each train?

*Melissa has 7 carriages, and Kathryn has 5.*

4 What do you need to know to solve the story problem? What do you need to know to find out how many more carriages Melissa has?

*I will take 5 carriages away from 7 carriages.*

5 How will you solve the story problem? How will you find out how many more carriages Melissa has?

6 Write a number sentence for this story problem on the blackboard: (7 − 5 = _____) Have the children copy the number sentence on their worksheets.

*I will compare the number of carriages Melissa has to the number of carriages Kathryn has. I will match the carriages and count to find out the number Melissa has left over.*

7 How could you use the picture to find your answer?

8　What do you think your answer will be? Will it be greater than 4?

9　Find your answer using the picture.

10　What did you guess your answer would be? Is it the same?

*Melissa has 2 more carriages than Kathryn.*

11　Give your answer in a sentence.

Follow a similar procedure with the story problems for Lesson I-9 listed below. You may want to do another problem together and then just read the remaining story problems to the children, letting them do the last few on their own. Encourage the children to use the pictures to help them solve the story problems. Let them color in their pictures at the end of the lesson.

**STORY PROBLEMS**

1　There were 9 dogs on our street. The Simpsons moved in last week. They have 2 dogs. How many dogs are on our street now?

2　Randy collected 13 acorns. He took the caps off 4. How many acorns still have their caps?

3　Jackie saw 12 penguins at the zoo. 4 were swimming, and the rest were waddling about on dry land. How many penguins were waddling about?

4　Martha collected 11 walnuts. She cracked the shells of 4 and ate the nuts inside. How many walnuts does Martha have left?

*Bonus*　Anne had 2 rows of red buttons on her new coat. There were 5 buttons in each row. She lost 1 button. How many buttons are on Anne's new coat now? (Use your crayons to draw the coat and the 2 rows of 5 red buttons.)

**ANSWERS
(For Student Problems)**

1　There are 11 dogs on your street now.

2　9 acorns still have their caps.

3　8 penguins were waddling about.

4　Martha has 7 walnuts left.

*Bonus*　There are 9 buttons on Anne's new coat.

Name_____

Sample Problem:

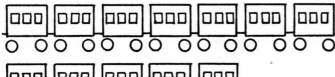

1.

2.

3.

4.

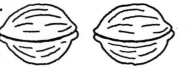

# Lesson I-10  Drawing Pictures of Story Problems

**PURPOSES**
- To draw a picture about each story problem by connecting dots.

- To state how the picture helps to solve the story problem.

- To review the steps of the major problem-solving approach.

**DIRECTIONS**

**1. Sample Problem**

Ask the children to look at the first dotted picture on their worksheet. (See Pictures for Lesson I-10 at the end of the lesson.) Tell the children the following story problem:

> Tom and Marcie went fishing and caught 8 fish altogether.
>
> They shared the fish they caught equally.
>
> How many fish did each one get?

**2. Children Draw a Picture of the Story Problem**

Ask the children to draw a line through the dots to make a picture of the fish.

*8*    1  How many fish did you draw?

*8*    2  How many fish did Tom and Marcie catch?

**3. Major Problem-Solving Approach**

Discuss the story problem with the children by asking them the following questions:

*Fish.*    1  What is the story problem about?

*How many fish did each one get?*    2  What is the question? What do you need to find out?

*Marcie and Tom caught 8 fish, and they shared them equally.*    3  What do you need to know to solve the story problem? What do you need to know to find out how many fish each one got?

*I will divide the fish in half; I will take turns giving a fish to Tom and a fish to Marcie.*

4 Look at your picture. How many fish did you draw?

How will you use your picture to find out how many fish each one got?

5 Write a number sentence for the story problem on the blackboard: (8 ÷ 2 = _____ ) Have the children copy the number sentence.

6 What do you think your answer will be? Will it be greater or less than 8?

*Note: You may have the students color Marcie's fish one color and Tom's another.*

7 Find the answer together by dividing the fish in half and complete the number sentence.

8 What did you guess the answer would be? Is it the same?

*Tom and Marcie got 4 fish each.*

9 Give your answer in a sentence.

Follow a similar procedure with the story problems listed below. First tell the children the story problem and then have them draw the picture by connecting all the dots. Encourage them to use their pictures to solve each story problem.

**STORY PROBLEMS**

1 There are 2 mother ducks in the pond. Each mother duck has 3 ducklings. How many ducks are there altogether?

2 James made 12 chocolate chip cookies. He shared them equally with Paul and Anne. How many cookies did each one get?

*Bonus* Sylvia bought a box of 12 crayons. She gave half to Marilyn. How many crayons does Sylvia have left? (Draw a picture of all the crayons and put an M on those she gave to Marilyn.)

**ANSWERS (For Student Problems)**

1 There are 8 ducks altogether.

2 Each child got 4 cookies.

*Bonus* Sylvia has 6 crayons left.

**Sample Problem:**

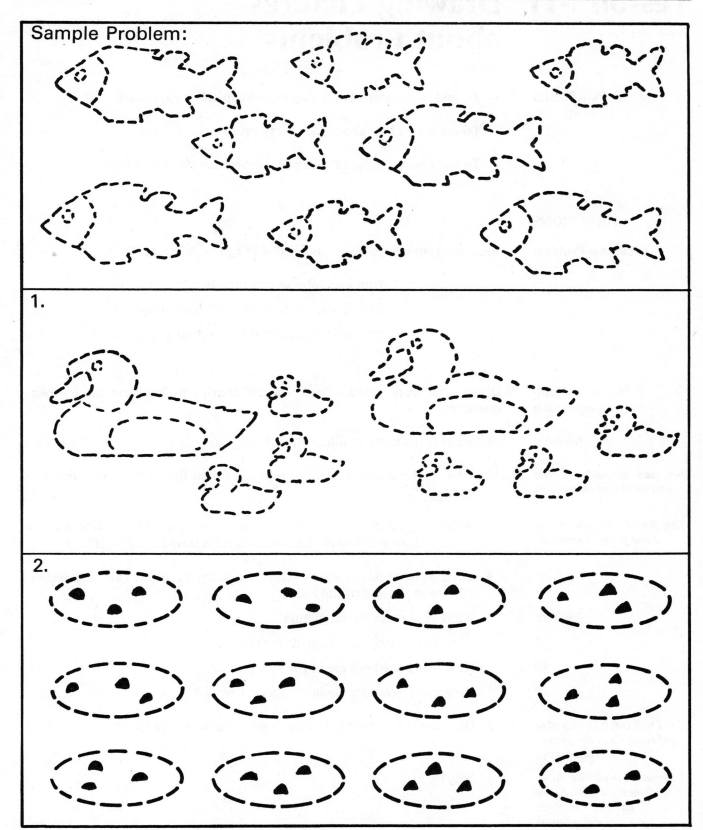

1.

2.

# Lesson I-11　Drawing Pictures about Problems

**PURPOSES**

- To review the steps of the major problem-solving approach.

- To draw a picture about each story problem.

- To state how the pictures helped to solve the story problems.

**DIRECTIONS**

**1. Sample Problem**

Read the following story problem slowly to the children:

> Tom and John went to the beach.
>
> Tom found 10 seashells, and John found 7.
>
> How many seashells did they find altogether?

**2. Major Problem-Solving Approach**

Discuss the story problem with the children by asking them the following questions:

*Seashells.*

1　What is the story problem about?

*How many seashells did Tom and John find altogether?*

2　What is the question? What do you want to find out to solve the story problem?

*Tom found 10 seashells, and John found 7 seashells.*

3　What do you need to know to solve the story problem? How will you find out how many seashells Tom and John found altogether?

4　Let's look at the picture about the story problem. (See the seashell picture at the end of the lesson.)

*Seashells.*

What do you see in the picture?

*2*

How many groups of seashells are there?

*10*

How many seashells are in the first group?

*7*

How many seashells are in the second group?

*I will count the number of seashells in the picture altogether.*

5　How can the picture help you to solve the story problem?

*Because the picture shows the 10 seashells Tom found and the 7 seashells John found.*

Why?

6  Write a number sentence for this story problem on the blackboard: (10 + 7 = _____) Have the children copy the number sentence on their worksheets.

7  What do you think your answer will be? Will it be greater than 10?

8  Add using your number sentence. What is your answer?

9  What did you guess your answer to be? Is it the same?

*Tom and John found 17 seashells altogether.*

10  Give your answer in a sentence.

Follow a similar procedure with the story problems listed below. However, get the children to draw their own pictures of the story problems. Encourage them to use their pictures to solve the story problems.

**STORY PROBLEMS**

1  Mary made 2 headbands with 8 feathers in each headband. How many feathers did she use altogether?

2  Tim's Mom has 2 key rings. There are 7 keys on one and 8 on the other. How many keys does Tim's Mom have altogether?

*Bonus*  Peter made 16 muffins. He ate 4. How many muffins does Peter have left?

**ANSWERS**
**(For Student Problems)**

1  Mary used 16 feathers altogether.

2  Tim's Mom has 15 keys altogether.

*Bonus*  Peter has 12 muffins left.

Name_____

## Sample:

**1.**

**2.**

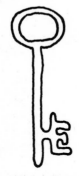

## Bonus:

# Lesson I-12 Making Graphs and Solving Story Problems

**PURPOSES**
- To play a game and record the scores on a graph.

- To develop story problems from the game.

- To solve the story problems by using the graph and the major problem-solving approach.

**MATERIALS NEEDED**
- Make a copy of the Graph for Lesson I-12 at the end of the lesson for each child.

- Also provide chalk and a bean bag.

**DIRECTIONS**

**1. Shapes Game** Take the children out into the school yard and draw the following shapes with chalk on the pavement:

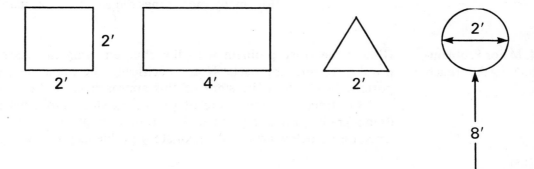

Draw a straight line between 8' and 10' from the shapes. You are now ready to start. The rules of the game are as follows:

1  Each child stands behind the line and throws the bean bag.

2  If the bean bag lands in a shape, the child records the score by making an X above the corresponding shape on his or her graph and gets another throw.

**3** If the bean bag lands outside a shape or on a line, the child records a "miss" on his or her graph, and the next child has a turn.

Continue the game until someone gets 7 points in one shape or 7 points in all the shapes. Encourage the children to record all their scores. Someone who has 7 misses is eliminated from the game.

**2. Discussion**

After the game, talk about what happened:

**1** How many squares/rectangles/triangles/circles did you hit?

**2** How many misses did you get?

**3** Who hit the most squares?

**4** What shape was the easiest to hit?

**3. Sample Problem**

Generate a story problem from the children's responses. Use a child's graph while telling a story problem. For example:

> Let's look at Regina's graph.
>
> She hit the square 5 times.
>
> She hit the rectangle 3 times.
>
> How many more times did she hit the square?

**4. Major Problem-Solving Approach**

Discuss the story problem with the children using the steps of the major problem-solving approach. Note specifically the main idea, questions, important facts, etc. (The steps of this approach are outlined in Chapter 1.)

Continue this procedure of generating story problems from the children's graphs. Encourage them to use their graphs to solve the story problems. Listed below are examples of story problems you could generate.

**SUGGESTED STORY PROBLEMS**

**1** Let's look at Sally's graph. Sally hit the triangle 3 times and the circle 7 times. How many more times did Sally hit the circle?

**2** Let's look at Joe's graph. Joe hit the square 6 times, the rectangle 3 times, the triangle twice, and the circle 7 times. What shape did Joe hit the most?

**3** Let's look at Sue's graph. Sue hit the square 5 times, the rectangle twice, the triangle 3 times, and the circle 7 times. How many hits did she get?

**4** Sue got 17 hits and 6 misses. How many more hits did she get than misses?

Name_____

## Shapes Game

| | | | | | |
|---|---|---|---|---|---|
| 7 | | | | | |
| 6 | | | | | |
| 5 | | | | | |
| 4 | | | | | |
| 3 | | | | | |
| 2 | | | | | |
| 1 | | | | | |
| | □ | ▭ | △ | ○ | miss |

# Lesson I-13  Solving Problems from Related Diagrams

PURPOSES
- To show the children how to use diagrams to help solve story problems.

- To review the major problem-solving approach.

MATERIALS NEEDED    Make a copy of the Diagrams for Lesson I-13 for each child.

DIRECTIONS

**1. Introduction and Discussion**

Tell the children to look at the top of their diagram sheet where they can see two groups of straight lines.

*7*  1  How many straight lines are there in the first group?

*5*  2  How many straight lines are there in the second group?

*12*  3  How many straight lines are there altogether?

A diagram is a very simple picture of something. The straight lines drawn here represent popsicle sticks.

**2. Sample Problem**

Read the following story problem slowly to the children:

> I had 7 popsicle sticks.
>
> The teacher gave me 5 more.
>
> How many popsicle sticks do I have now?

**3. Major Problem-Solving Approach**

Discuss the story problem with the children by asking them the following questions:

*Popsicle sticks.*

1  What is the story problem about?

*How many popsicle sticks do I have now?*

2  What is the question? What do you want to find out to solve the story problem?

*I had 7 popsicle sticks, and the teacher gave me 5 more.*

3  What do you need to know to solve the story problem?

*Add the number of popsicle sticks I had in the beginning to the number of popsicle sticks the teacher gave me.*

4  Tell in your own words what you need to do to solve the problem.

5  Write a number sentence for this story problem on the blackboard: (7 + 5 = _____) Have the children copy the number sentence.

*Each straight line represents a popsicle stick. The first group of 7 lines represents the 7 popsicle sticks I had in the beginning, and the second group of 5 straight lines represents the 5 popsicle sticks the teacher gave me. If I count the number of straight lines in the diagram altogether, I will find the answer.*

6  How could you use the diagram to find your answer?

7  What do you think your answer will be? Will it be less than or greater than 7?

8  Find your answer using the diagram.

9  What did you think your answer would be? Is it the same?

*I have 12 popsicle sticks now.*

10  How many popsicle sticks do you have now? Give your answer in a sentence.

Continue this procedure with the following five story problems. You may want to do one more together, and then let the children do the last few story problems on their own (after the problems have been read aloud to them). Encourage the children to use the diagrams to help them to solve the story problems and to compute their answer by counting.

**STORY PROBLEMS**

1  Jim has 3 baseballs, Cecile has 2 baseballs, and Robert has only 1 baseball. How many baseballs do they have altogether?

2  There were 4 men and 5 women at a meeting. How many people were at the meeting?

3  Anne picked 3 daisies, Margaret picked 3 daisies, and Jonathan picked 2 daisies. How many daisies did the children pick altogether?

4   Sam read 4 books last week, Joe read 3 books, and Tom read 2 books. How many books did the boys read altogether?

*Bonus*   Jane made a chocolate cake for tea. Jane ate 3 slices of the cake, Sue ate 2 slices, Roger ate 4 slices, and Dave ate 3 slices. When they had finished eating, there was no more cake left. How many slices was the cake cut into? (Draw a diagram with 1 mark for each slice of cake.)

**ANSWERS**
**(For Student Problems)**

1   The children have 6 baseballs altogether.

2   9 people were at the meeting.

3   The children picked 8 daisies altogether.

4   The boys read 9 books altogether.

*Bonus*   The cake was cut into 12 slices.

Name_____

Sample:

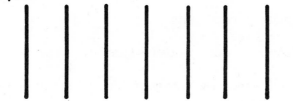

---

**1.**

---

**2.**

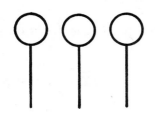 

---

**3.**

---

**4.**

# Lesson I-14  Activity-Based Story Problems

PURPOSES

- For the children to make potato prints.

- For the children to compose story problems based on the activity.

- For the children to solve their own story problems using the steps of the major problem-solving approach.

MATERIALS NEEDED

- Medium-size potatoes, cleaned, cut in half, and dried.

- Paint and brushes or ink pads.

- Knives, felt pens, paper.

- Soft rags for drying the potatoes.

DIRECTIONS

**1. Children Make Potato Prints**

Have all the materials available for the children and show them how to prepare their potatoes to make an interesting print.

1  Draw a design on your potato with a felt pen.

2  Cut away the parts of the potato that lie outside your design.

3  Blot the surface with a soft rag to dry the potato.

4  Paint the raised surface, or use ink pads, and press face down on your paper to make a potato print.

Encourage the children to make more designs and to make a lot of prints with their designs.

**2. Discussion**

When everyone has finished, talk with the children about what they did.

1  How many designs did you make?

2  What kinds of designs did you make?

3  How many prints did you make of each design?

4  What colors did you use?

**3. Sample Problem**   Generate a story problem from the children's responses. For example:

Jerry made 5 prints with one design and 8 prints with another.
How many prints did Jerry make altogether?

**4. Children Compose a Story Problem**   Ask each child to make up a story problem about what he or she did. Encourage them by asking leading questions such as:

1   How many designs did you make?

2   How many prints did you make with each design?

If the children tell stories that are not story problems, help them turn their stories into story problems. For example, if a child says, "I made 8 blue prints and 7 red prints," you could respond as follows:

*It asks a question.*   1   What does a story problem always do?

*No.*   2   Does "I made 8 blue prints and 7 red prints" ask a question?

*How many prints did I make altogether? What color prints did I make the most? How many more blue prints did I make?*   3   Can you add a question to make a story problem?

**5. Major Problem-Solving Approach**   Repeat some of the children's story problems and solve them together, using the steps of the major problem-solving approach. (See Chapter 1 for details if necessary.)

At the end of the lesson, help the children write down their story problems.

# Lesson I-15    Story Problems from Pictures

- For the children to compose and solve story problem based on pictures.

**DIRECTIONS**

**1. Introduction and Discussion**

Ask the children to look at the first picture on their worksheets. Discuss the picture with them in the following manner:

*10*    1   How many kites do you see?

*2*    2   How many groups of kites do you see?

*5*    3   How many kites are there in each group?

4   I want to make up a story problem about these kites. I have a set of 10 kites that is made up of two groups of 5, so I could make up a story problem like this one:

> There were 10 kites in the toy shop.
>
> 5 were sold.
>
> How many are left?

**2. Children Compose a Story Problem**

Ask the children to make up a story problem about the 10 kites.

**3. Major Problem-Solving Approach**

Repeat the children's story problems and solve them. If the children have difficulty in solving their story problems, use the steps of the major problem-solving approach. (See Chapter 1 for details and/or make up a chart of the steps to follow: Main Idea, Question, Important Facts, etc.).

Follow this procedure with the remaining pictures. Encourage the children to make up a story problem without first giving them a sample problem. Help the children write their story problems on their worksheets at the end of the lesson.

Name_____

## Sample:

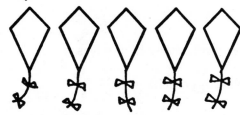 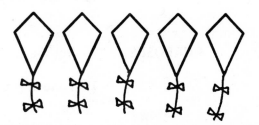

1.

2.

3.

4.

5.

# Lesson I-16  Reviewing the Major Problem-Solving Approach

PURPOSES
- For the children to write a number sentence by themselves.

- To review the major problem-solving approach.

DIRECTIONS

**1. Sample Problem**

Read the following story problem slowly with the children:

> Joan made 9 spool dolls.
>
> Dave made 7 spool dolls.
>
> How many spool dolls did they make altogether?

**2. Major Problem-Solving Approach**

Discuss the story problem with the children by asking them the following questions:

*Spool dolls.*

1  What is the story problem about?

*How many spool dolls did Joan and Dave make altogether?*

2  What is the question? What do you need to find out?

*Joan made 9 spool dolls, and Dave made 7.*

3  What do you need to know to solve the story problem?

*I will add the number of spool dolls Joan made to the number of spool dolls Dave made.*

4  How will you solve the story problem?

*9 and 7*

5  What numbers will you use?

*Add.*

Will you add or subtract?

$9 + 7 =$ _____

Write a number sentence for this story problem.

6  What do you think your answer will be? Will it be greater or less than 9?

7  Compute the answer together and complete the number sentence.

8  What did you guess your answer would be? Is it the same?

*Joan and Dave made 16
spool dolls altogether.*

9   Give your answer in a sentence.

Follow a similar procedure with the story problems for Lesson I-16 on the next page. You may wish to do one or two problems together and then just read the remaining story problems with the children, letting them solve them on their own. If desired, the children may use objects to represent the problem situations, and/or simple pictures or diagrams may be utilized.

**ANSWERS
(For Student Problems)**

1   Joan needed 18 spools to make 3 spool dolls.

2   Andy and Betsy made 21 jack-o'-lanterns altogether.

3   Tina collected 21 leaves altogether.

4   Sue took 20 photos altogether.

5   There are 18 brass buttons on Dick's coat altogether.

*Bonus*   There are 2 cherries left.

**LESSON 1-16**                     Name_____

**SAMPLE PROBLEM**

Joan made 9  . Dave made 7
 . How many spool dolls did

they make altogether?

---

| | |
|---|---|
| 1  Joan used 6 ⊙ to make a 🪆 . How many spools did she need to make 3 spool dolls? | 2  Andy made 10 🎃 for the party. Betsy made 11 🎃 . How many jack-o'-lanterns did they make altogether? |
| 3  Tina collected 9 oak 🍂 and 12 maple 🍁 . How many leaves did she collect altogether? | 4  Sue got a 📷 for her birthday. She took 8 🖼 at her party and 12 🖼 at the zoo. How many photos did she take altogether? |
| 5  Dick has 12 brass ⊙⊙ on the front of his 👕 and 3 brass ⊙⊙ on each 🧤 . How many brass buttons are there on Dick's coat altogether? | *Bonus*  There were 20 🍒 in the fruit 🥣 . Danny ate 11 🍒 . Joe ate 7 🍒 . How many cherries are left? |

# Chapter 4

# GRADE 2
# PROBLEM-SOLVING
# LESSONS
## (LEVEL ⊔)

By the time children enter the second grade, they are ready for the challenge of solving more abstract and complex problems—provided that the problems are meaningful and interesting to them and they have already developed certain prerequisite skills. The lessons for this level are designed to develop children's skills for solving such problems. For this purpose, the major problem-solving approach is introduced in the first three lessons and developed throughout the series.

The supporting techniques (using pictures, drawing, developing language and math vocabulary, composing problems, etc.), as developed in the previous chapters, are also augmented here by certain additional techniques such as solving problems with diagrams, drawing diagrams, and building tables. These new techniques will help children to develop the skills necessary to solve the more difficult problems that are introduced at this level, including some with two steps.

Each lesson begins with plans for the teacher, including suggested questions and responses for a sample problem; then a copy of the student page follows immediately. This arrangement provides the teacher with immediate access to the Purposes, Directions, and Answers for the lesson as well as a copy of the student page. Any student problem pages or supplemental problem-solving aids (such as pictures and charts) may be duplicated in quantities necessary for the teacher's own classroom use.

Although the lessons have been designed primarily to develop problem-solving skills, they also provide computation practice appropriate for children working at the second-grade level. Problems 1 and 2 for each lesson provide easy computations, while Problems 3, 4, and 5 are more difficult. The bonus problem might be completed only by the more advanced students. In addition, the lessons are sequenced such that a student who is not working up to grade level may be exposed to the same problem-solving approach and techniques, but with easier problems, by being assigned the Grade 1 (Level I) problems, and a student who is able to do advanced work could be assigned the problems from Grade 3 (Level ⊔).

# Lesson L-1 Introducing the Major Problem-Solving Approach

**PURPOSE**

- To introduce the children to the initial steps of the major problem-solving approach by:

  1 Finding the main idea in the problem.

  2 Determining what is wanted.

  3 Determining the important facts in the problem.

**DIRECTIONS**

**1. Sample Problem**

Give each child a copy of the student problem page for Lesson L-1 and read the following problem slowly with the children:

> Emily had a box of 12 crayons.
>
> She lost 4 crayons.
>
> How many crayons does Emily have now?

**2. Major Problem-Solving Approach**

Discuss the problem with the children by asking them the following questions:

*Crayons.*

1 What is the problem about?

*How many crayons Emily has now.*

2 What do you want to find out to solve the problem?

*Emily had 12 crayons, and she lost 4 of them.*

3 What do you need to know to solve the problem?

Follow a similar procedure with the problems for Lesson L-1 on the student problem page. For some children it will help to draw a picture of the situation. You may want to do another problem together and then let the children do the last few problems on their own.

It is not necessary for the children to solve the problems in this lesson; however, if they wish to do so, it is permissible. Discuss the problems with the children when they have finished.

**OPTIONAL ANSWERS**
**(For Student Problems)**

*Sample*   Emily has 8 crayons now.

1   The girls picked 14 flowers altogether.

2   16 birds were left on the telephone wire.

3   Tom has 19 marbles now.

4   Sandy made 21 muffins altogether.

5   Jim and Trina are feeding 16 rabbits altogether.

*Bonus*   Sally put 8 cards on the table.

Name_____

**SAMPLE PROBLEM**

Emily had a 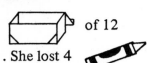 of 12

. She lost 4 .

How many crayons does Emily

have now?

---

1  Mary picked 5 . Anne picked 9

. How many flowers did they

pick altogether?

---

2  19 were resting on the

telephone wire. 3 flew away.

How many birds were left on the telephone

wire?

---

3  Tom played with his sister. He

has 11 , and he won 8 more. How

many marbles does he have now? (You may

want to draw a picture of the marbles.)

---

4  Sandy made for the school

potluck. She made 9 banana

and 12 raisin . How many muffins

did Sandy make altogether?

---

5  Jim and Trina are feeding their .

Jim has 9 , and Trina has 7

. How many rabbits are they

feeding altogether?

---

*Bonus*  Sally received 20 for her birth-

day. She hung 12 on her BULLETIN BOARD

and put the rest on a . How

many birthday cards did she put on

the table?

---

# Lesson L-2  Using the Major Problem-Solving Approach

PURPOSE
- To review and expand the steps of the major problem-solving approach by:

  1  Finding the main idea in the problem.

  2  Determining what is wanted, i.e., the question.

  3  Determining the important facts in the problem.

  4  Stating how to solve the problem.*

  5  Writing a number sentence for the problem.*

  6  Computing the answer.*

  7  Stating the answer sentence.*

## DIRECTIONS

**1. Sample Problem**

Give each child a copy of the student problem page for Lesson L-2 and read the following problem slowly with the children:

> Tom has 13 toy cars.
>
> Kitty has 6 toy cars.
>
> How many toy cars do they have altogether?

**2. Major Problem-Solving Approach**

Lead the children to a solution of the problem using the following types of questions:

*Note: At this stage it is important that the children use each step when working through problems with you. When working on their own, they may leave out steps, but they should know what the steps are so that they can refer back if they have any difficulty.*

*Toy cars.*  1  What is the problem about?

---

*Steps 4 through 7 are being introduced here for the first time.

*How many cars do they have altogether?*

2 What is the question? What do you want to find out to solve the problem?

*Tom has 13 toy cars, and Kitty has 6 toy cars.*

3 What do you need to know to solve the problem?

*Add the number of cars Tom has to the number of cars Kitty has.*

4 How will you solve the problem? What will you do to solve the problem?

For some children an illustration of Tom's 13 cars and Kitty's 6 may be a help.

$13 + 6 =$ _____

5 Write a number sentence for this problem.

6 Add the two numbers together. What is your answer?

*They have 19 cars altogether.*

7 Give your answer in a sentence.

Follow a similar procedure with the following six problems for Lesson ∟-2 on the next page. You may want to do another problem together to give the children practice at using the steps. Then read the remaining problems with the children, letting them try the last few on their own. They may utilize objects or simple drawings to represent problem situations if they wish. Discuss the problems with the children when they have finished.

**ANSWERS**
**(For Student Problems)**

1 Rob has 12 books left.

2 9 goldfish are left.

3 Mary and John picked 17 roses altogether.

4 There are 14 animals in Andy's picture.

5 There are 24 children going on the trip.

*Bonus* Sue had 23 cookies in the beginning.

**LESSON L-2**

Name_____

**SAMPLE PROBLEM**

Tom has 13 toy 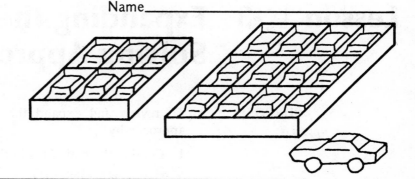 .

Kitty has 6 toy .

How many toy cars do they have

altogether?

---

1  Rob had 15 . He lost 3 on his way to school. How many books does Rob have left?

2  There were 15 in the aquarium. 6 died. How many goldfish are left?

---

3  There is a growing in Mary's garden. Mary picked 12 , and John picked 5 . How many roses did they pick altogether?

4  Andy drew a picture of 5 and 9 . How many animals are in Andy's picture?

---

5  The are going on a trip. 19 are going in the SCHOOL BUS , and 5 are going by car. How many children are going on the trip altogether?

*Bonus*  Sue has a bag of for lunch. She ate 5 and gave 6 to her friend Mary. Now she has 12 left. How many cookies did Sue have in the beginning?

---

# Lesson L-3 Expanding the Major Problem-Solving Approach

**PURPOSE**

- To review and expand the initial steps of the major problem-solving approach by:

  1 Finding the main idea in the problem.

  2 Determining what is wanted, i.e., the question.

  3 Determining the important facts in the problem.

  4 Stating how to solve the problem.

  5 Writing a number sentence for the problem.

  6 Estimating the answer.*

  7 Computing the answer.

  8 Comparing the estimation with the answer.*

  9 Stating the answer sentence.

**DIRECTIONS**

**1. Sample Problem**

Give the children a copy of the student problem page for Lesson L-3 and read the following problem slowly with them:

Dan had 22 felt pens for coloring.

His little brother lost 8 of them.

How many felt pens does Dan have left?

**2. Major-Problem Solving Approach**

Discuss the problem with the children by asking them the following questions:

*Felt pens.*

1 What is the problem about?

*How many felt pens does Dan have left?*

2 What is the question? What do you need to find out?

*Dan had 22 felt pens, and his little brother lost 8 of them.*

3 What do you need to know to solve the problem?

---

*Steps 6 and 8 are being introduced here for the first time. The children have now been introduced to all the steps needed for solving word problems.

*I will take away the number of felt pens Dan's little brother lost from the number of felt pens Dan had in the beginning.*

$22 - 8 =$ _____

4 How will you solve the problem? What will you do to solve the problem? It may also help to illustrate the 22 pens and then to X out the 8 lost.

5 Write a number sentence for this problem.

6 What do you think your answer will be? Will it be more or less than 22?

7 Subtract and fill in the number sentence. What is your answer?

8 What did you guess your answer would be? Is it the same?

*Dan has 14 pens left.*

9 Give your answer in a sentence.

Follow a similar procedure with the following six problems for Lesson L-2 on the student problem page. You may want to do another problem together to give the children practice at using all of the steps. Then read the remaining problems with the children, letting them solve them on their own. If helpful, they may utilize manipulatives and/or simple drawings of problem situations. Discuss all the problems with the children when they have finished.

**ANSWERS**
**(For Student Problems)**

1 Mary spent $24 altogether.

2 There are 18 candles altogether.

3 Alice received 26 get well cards altogether.

4 Each child got 3 slices of cake.

5 Angela collected 23 shells altogether.

*Bonus* Each child got 5 cookies.

**SAMPLE PROBLEM**

Dan had 22 felt  for coloring. His little brother lost 8 of them. How many felt pens does Dan have left?

Giant Pen Pack
22 COLORS

---

1  Mary bought a ⬭ for $15 and a 〰 for $9. How much money did she spend altogether?

2  In Bruce's dining room there are 3 ⬭ with 6 ⵜⵜ in each. How many candles are there altogether?

3  Alice fell out of a 🌳 and broke her 💪. She received 12 GET WELL from the 👫 in her school and 14 GET WELL from 👫 on her block. How many get well cards did Alice receive altogether?

4  There were 6 👫 at Sally's birthday party. She cut her 🎂 into 18 slices and divided them equally among 👫. How many slices of cake did each child get?

5  Angela went to the beach and collected 12 clam 🐚 and 11 mussel 🐚. How many shells did she collect altogether?

**Bonus**  John had a packet of 20 🍪. He divided them equally among Thomas, Amy, Sue, and himself. How many cookies did each child get?

---

# Lesson ∟-4  Using Mathematical Vocabulary

PURPOSES
- To instruct the children in how to solve problems containing the following mathematical vocabulary: *most*, *least*, and *equals*.

- To provide the children with further instruction in the steps of the major problem-solving approach.

DIRECTIONS

**1. Sample Problem**

Give each child a copy of the student problem page for Lesson ∟-4 and read the following problem slowly with the children:

> Linda has 19 colored pens.
>
> Diana has 17 colored pens.
>
> Who has the most colored pens?

**2. Major Problem-Solving Approach**

Discuss the problem with the children by asking them the following questions:

*Colored pencils.*

1 What is the problem about?

*Who has the most colored pencils.*

2 What is the question? What do you want to find out to solve the problem?

*Linda has 19 pencils, and Diana has 17 pencils.*

3 What do you need to know to solve the problem?

*Most.*

4 Which word in the problem tells you how to solve it?

*Because most means the greatest number.*

   Why?

*By comparing.*

5 How will you solve the problem? How will you find out who has the *most*?

   A drawing showing 19 pens and 17 pens may be helpful.

*19 > 17*

6 Can you write a number sentence for this problem?

*Linda has the most colored pencils.*

7 Give your answer in a sentence.

Follow a similar procedure with the problems for Lesson L-4. You may want to do one or two more together to give the children practice at following the steps and to explain the mathematical terms "least" and "equals" to them. Read the problems with the children, but let them do the last few on their own. They may make use of simple drawings and/or manipulatives to help them if they wish. Discuss all the problems with the children when they have finished.

**ANSWERS**
**(For Student Problems)**

1 Joan has the least storybooks.

2 No, there is not an equal number of pictures in both rooms.

3 February has the least days.

4 Robert needs 2 more pennies.

5 Jenny ate the most candies.

*Bonus* Mary should give Dave 1 more flower.

**LESSON L-4**

Name_____

**SAMPLE PROBLEM**

Linda has 19 colored  . Diana has 17

colored _____ . Who has

the most colored pens?

---

| | |
|---|---|
| 1  Sally has 21 [story book] . Joan has 19 [story book] . Who has the least storybooks? | 2  There are 17 [picture] in one room. There are 18 [picture] in another room. Is there an equal number of pictures in both rooms? |
| 3  There are 12 months in the year. January has 31 days, and February has 28 days. Which month has the least days? | 4  Sue has 15 (penny) , and Robert has 13 (penny) . How many more (penny) does Robert need so the number of pennies he has equals the number of pennies Sue has? |
| 5  Tim and Jenny had 16 (candies) . Tim ate 7 (candies) , and Jenny ate the rest. Who ate the most candies? | *Bonus*  Mary and Dave picked 16 (flower) . Mary took 9 (flower) and gave the rest to Dave. How many more flowers should Mary give Dave so that the number of flowers she has will equal the number Dave has? |

# Lesson L-5  Finding Key Words

**PURPOSES**

- To provide instruction in locating and relating these key words to their appropriate operations:

  | "left" | — | subtraction |
  |--------|---|-------------|
  | "in all" | + | addition |
  | "altogether" | + | addition |

- To further instruct the children in the steps of the major problem-solving approach.

**DIRECTIONS**

**1. Sample Problem**

Give each child a copy of the student problem page for Lesson L-5 and read the following problem slowly with the children:

> Rover had 17 dog biscuits.
>
> He ate 13 of them.
>
> How many dog biscuits does Rover have left?

**2. Major Problem-Solving Approach**

Discuss the problem with the children by asking them the following questions:

*Dog biscuits.*

1  What is the problem about?

*How many dog biscuits does Rover have left?*

2  What do you want to find out?

*Rover had 17 dog biscuits, and he ate 13 of them.*

3  What do you need to know to solve it?

*I will subtract or take away the number of dog biscuits Rover ate from the number he had in the beginning.*

4  How will you solve the problem?

You may want to draw 17 dog biscuits and then mark out 13.

*Left.*

4  Is there any word in the problem that lets you know you must subtract to find your answer?

*Because I have to take away to find out how many are left.*

Why?

138

Have the children locate, underline, and discuss the meanings of the key words *altogether, in all,* and *left* in Problems 1, 2, and 3 on the next page. Then let them solve the problems by themselves. Use the major problem-solving approach if the children have any difficulty. They may also use manipulatives or simple drawings to represent the problem situations if this proves helpful. Continue this procedure with the remaining problems for Lesson └-5.

**ANSWERS**
**(For Student Problems)**

1  Sally spent 28¢ altogether.

2  John and Mary sharpened 24 pencils in all.

3  Karen has 10¢ left.

4  Ellen has 14 sticks of chalk left.

5  The children caught 15 fish in all.

*Bonus*  The children used 21 daisies altogether.

**LESSON L-5**

Name_____

**SAMPLE PROBLEM**

Rover  had 17 🦴

He ate 13 of them. How many dog

biscuits does Rover have left?

---

1 Sally paid 18¢ for 🍬🍬 and 10¢ for

a ⊖ . How much money did

Sally spend altogether?

2 John and Mary were asked to sharpen

✏️ . John sharpened 15

✏️ and Mary sharpened 9

✏️ . How many pencils did

they sharpen in all?

---

3 Karen had 30¢. She bought an 🍎

for 20¢. How much money does Karen

have left?

4 Ellen had 25 sticks of ⬭ . She gave

11 sticks to her sister. How many sticks

of chalk does Ellen have left?

---

5 Danny, Roberta, and Luke went fishing.

They caught 5 🐟 each. How

many fish did they catch in all?

*Bonus* Tom, Sue, and Marion made 3 flower

 . They used 7  in each

 . How many daisies did they

use altogether?

---

**140**

# Lesson └-6   Problem Solving and Vocabulary Development

PURPOSES

- To introduce the children to problems containing two different sets, both of which belong to a larger universal set:

| | |
|---|---|
| boys and girls | — children |
| oranges and apples | — fruit |
| trout and sunfish | — fish |
| tables and chairs | — furniture |
| sparrows and pigeons | — birds |
| dogs and cats | — pets |
| daisies, bluebells, and buttercups | — flowers |

- To continue to use the major problem-solving approach.

## DIRECTIONS

**1. Introduction and Discussion**

Ask the children the following questions:

1   Are there any boys in the group?

2   Are there any girls in the group?

*Children.*

3   There are girls and boys in the group. Is there one word we can use for girls and boys?

**2. Sample Problem**

Give each child a copy of the student problem page for Lesson └-6 and read the following problem slowly to the children:

> 15 girls and 9 boys were playing a game.
>
> How many children were playing together?

**3. Major Problem-Solving Approach**

Discuss the problem with the children by asking them the following questions:

*Children playing.*

1   What is the problem about?

*How many children were playing together?*

2   What do you want to find out to solve the problem? What is the question?

141

*15 girls and 9 boys were playing.*

3   What do you need to know to solve the problem?

*Add the number of girls and boys together.*

4   How will you solve the problem?

Why?

A stick figure drawing of the 15 girls and 9 boys may be helpful.

*Because the number of girls plus the number of boys will equal the total number of children.*

*15 + 9 = _____*

5   Write a number sentence for this problem.

6   What do you think your answer will be? Will it be more or less than 15?

7   Add the two numbers together. What is your answer?

8   What did you guess your answer would be? Is it the same?

*There were 24 children playing together.*

9   Give your answer in a sentence.

Complete the problems on the student problem page in a similar manner. Talk about each of the sets first and their relationship to a larger universal set. Discuss all the problems with the children at the end of the lesson.

ANSWERS
(For Student Problems)

1   Mary bought 23 pieces of fruit altogether.

2   The children caught 25 fish altogether.

3   There are 22 pieces of furniture altogether.

4   Mandy fed 23 birds altogether.

5   There are 26 pets altogether.

*Bonus*   Frank used 28 flowers altogether.

**SAMPLE PROBLEM**

15 girls and 9 boys were playing

a game. How many children were

playing altogether?

| | |
|---|---|
| 1  Mary bought 18 oranges and 5 apples. How many pieces of fruit did she buy altogether? | 2  Jamie, Dick, and Sally went fishing every weekend last summer. They caught 6 trout and 19 sunfish. How many fish did they catch altogether? |
| 3  There are 2 tables with 10 chairs around each table. How many pieces of furniture are there altogether? | 4  Mandy fed 12 parrots and 11 finches some bird seed. How many birds did she feed altogether? |
| 5  There are 7 dogs and 19 cats in the pet store. How many pets are there altogether? | *Bonus*  Frank made a bouquet of flowers with 11 daisies, 12 roses, and 5 petunias. How many flowers did he use altogether? |

# Lesson ∟-7    Oral Presentation of Nature Problems

<table>
<tr><td>PURPOSES</td><td>

- To develop the children's listening skills by reading to them simple oral problems, which they will solve mentally without the use of paper and pencil.

- To review the major problem-solving approach when presenting oral problems to children.

</td></tr>
</table>

## DIRECTIONS

**1. Introduction and Discussion**

Talk about spiders and flies with the children.

*In their webs.*

1  Where do spiders live?

*They spin a web.*

2  How do they build their homes?

*The flies get stuck in the spider's sticky web.*

3  How do they catch flies?

**2. Sample Problem**

Tell the children that you are going to read a problem to them and you want them to tell you what the problem is about and what the question is:

17 flies got caught in the spider's web.

3 flies escaped, and the spider ate the rest.

How many flies did the spider eat?

**3. Major Problem-Solving Approach**

After the first reading, ask the children:

*Flies.*

1  What is the problem about?

*How many flies did the spider eat?*

2  What is the question?

## 4. Continuing the Major Problem-Solving Approach

Reread the problem once again and ask the children:

*17 flies got caught in the spider's web, and 3 escaped.*

3  What do you need to know to solve the problem?

*Take away the number of flies that escaped from the number of flies that got caught.*

4  How will you solve the problem?

5  Do this subtraction in your head without writing anything down on your paper.

6  Write only the answer on your paper.

*The spider ate 14 flies.*

7  Give your answer in a sentence.

Tell the children that you are going to read six more problems to them. (The children do not need to receive copies of the student problem page for Lesson ∟-7; however, this is at the option of the classroom teacher.) The first time, they should listen to find out what the problem is about and what the question is. The second time, they should listen carefully for the important facts they need to know to solve the problem, decide how they will solve the problem, and think out the answer in their heads. They should write only the answer on their papers.

## ANSWERS
### (For Student Problems)

1  There are 12 flies left.

2  The honeybee collected nectar from 17 flowers.

3  Dan and James got 18 mosquito bites altogether.

4  There are 18 caterpillars altogether.

5  The mother ducks have 18 ducklings altogether.

*Bonus*  There are 17 frogs now.

LESSON L-7

Name_____

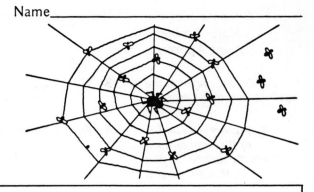

**SAMPLE PROBLEM**

17 flies got caught in the spider's

web. 3 escaped, and the spider ate

the rest. How many flies did the

spider eat?

| | |
|---|---|
| 1   There were 20 flies buzzing around the room. Mary killed 8 with a swat. How many flies are left? | 2   The honeybee collected nectar from 9 fuchsia flowers and 8 daffodils before flying back to its hive. How many flowers did the honeybee collect nectar from? |
| 3   Dan and James went camping last weekend. Dan got 7 mosquito bites and James got 11. How many mosquito bites did they get altogether? | 4   There are 9 caterpillars on one tree and 9 on another. How many caterpillars are there altogether? |
| 5   There are 3 mother ducks in the pond. Each mother duck has 6 ducklings. How many ducklings do they have altogether? | *Bonus*   There were 7 frogs and 20 tadpoles in the pond. 10 of the tadpoles became frogs. How many frogs are there now? |

146

# Lesson L-8   Music Shop Problems Presented Orally

**PURPOSES**

- To develop the children's ability to discriminate when finding out the prices of the musical instruments from a given price list.

- To develop the children's listening skills by reading simple oral problems to them, which they will solve mentally.

- To review the major problem-solving approach.

**DIRECTIONS**

**1. Introduction**

Give each child a copy of the price list (see Price List for Lesson L-8) and discuss it with them:

1  What instruments do you see?

2  How much do they cost?

**2. Sample Problem**

Read the following problem to them:

> Terry bought 2 sheets of music.
>
> How much money did Terry spend?

**3. Major Problem-Solving Approach**

*Buying sheet music.*

*How much money did Terry spend?*

Ask the children the following questions:

1  What is the problem about?

2  What is the question?

**4. Continue the Major Problem-Solving Approach**

Reread the problem once again and ask the children:

*The price of one sheet of music and that Terry bought 2 sheets.*

3  What do you need to know to solve the problem?

*I will add the price of one sheet of music together twice; or I will multiply the price of one sheet of music by 2.*

4  How will you solve the problem? What will you do to solve the problem?

*By looking at the price list.*

5  How will you find out how much a sheet of music costs?

6  Do the addition or multiplication in your head and write only your answer on the paper.

*Terry spent 20¢.*

7  Give your answer in a sentence.

Tell the children that you are going to read six more problems to them. The students do not need to receive copies of the student problem page for Lesson L-8; however, this is at the option of the classroom teacher. The first time, they should listen to find out what the problem is about and listen carefully for the question. On the second reading, they must listen for the important facts they need to know to solve the problem and use the price list to find out the prices of the musical instruments.

**ANSWERS (For Student Problems)**

1  Roger has $2 left.

2  Alice and Marty spent $12 altogether.

3  Two pairs of drumsticks cost Alice $4.

4  Lyn spent 50¢.

5  Joe has $2 left.

*Bonus*  John will have $10 left if he buys a guitar.

Name_____

**SAMPLE PROBLEM**

Terry bought 2 sheets of music. How

much money did Terry spend?

| | |
|---|---|
| 1  Roger had $8. He bought a drum. How much money does Roger have left? | 2  Alice and Marty each bought a drum. How much did they spend altogether? |
| 3  Alice bought 2 pairs of drumsticks in case she lost one. How much did 2 pairs of drumsticks cost her? | 4  Lyn bought 5 sheets of music. How much money did she spend? |
| 5  Joe had $10. He bought a drum and a pair of drumsticks. How much money does Joe have left? | *Bonus*  John has $60. How much money will he have left if he buys a guitar? |

Name_____

# Music Shop

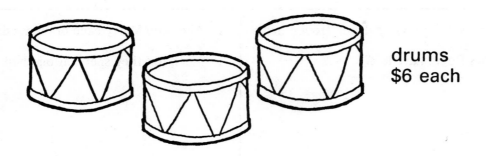

drums
$6 each

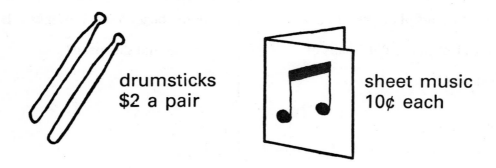

drumsticks
$2 a pair

sheet music
10¢ each

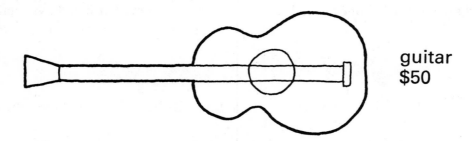

guitar
$50

# Lesson └-9  Using Mathematical Vocabulary

PURPOSES

- To instruct the children in how to solve problems using the following mathematical vocabulary: *half, double, twice.*

- To review the major problem-solving approach.

## DIRECTIONS

**1. Sample Problem**

Give each child a copy of the student problem page for Lesson └-9 and read the following problem slowly with them:

> Tom has 8 shirts.
>
> Joe has *half* as many.
>
> How many shirts does Joe have?

**2. Major Problem-Solving Approach**

Discuss the problem with the children by asking them the following questions:

*Shirts.*

1  What is the problem about?

*How many shirts does Joe have?*

2  What is the question? What do you need to find out to solve the problem?

*Tom has 8 shirts, and Joe has* half *as many.*

3  What do you need to know to solve the problem?

*Half.*

*Because* half *tells me to divide into 2 equal parts.*

4  What word in the problem tells you how to solve it?

Why?

Underline the word *half* in the problem.

*I will divide the number of shirts Tom has by 2.*

5  How will you solve the problem? What will you do to solve the problem?

This might be done by using 8 objects or a picture of 8 shirts and separating them into 2 equal groups.

*8 ÷ 2 = _____*

6  Write a number sentence for the problem.

7  What do you think your answer will be? Will it be less than 8?

8  Find your answer and complete the number sentence.

9  What did you guess your answer would be? Is it the same?

*Joe has 4 shirts.*

10  Give your answer in a sentence.

Follow a similar procedure with the remaining problems for Lesson L-9 on the next page. You may wish to do another problem together to explain the mathematical terms *twice* and *double* to the children. Discuss all the problems with them when they have finished.

**ANSWERS**
**(For Student Problems)**

1  Sam has 6 plants.

2  They drink 8 cartons of milk in Mabel's house in a week.

3  Mary needs to make 12 muffins altogether.

4  Andy counted 5 ducks.

5  There were 20 rainy days.

*Bonus*  Mark still has the most storybooks.

**LESSON L-9**

Name_____

**SAMPLE PROBLEM**

Tom has 8 shirts. Joe has half as
many. How many shirts does Joe
have?

| | |
|---|---|
| **1** Robin has 3 flowering plants in her house. Sam has twice as many. How many plants does Sam have? (You may want to draw a picture.) | **2** In Brian's house they drink 4 cartons of milk a week. In Mabel's house they drink double that amount in a week. How many cartons of milk do they drink in Mabel's house in a week? |
| **3** Mary is making muffins for a potluck. She has made 6 already but she needs twice as many so that there will be enough for everyone. How many muffins does Mary need to make altogether? | **4** Rob counted 10 ducks in the pond. His little brother Andy only counted half that many ducks. How many ducks did Andy count? |
| **5** There were 10 sunny days last month and double that many rainy days. How many rainy days were there? | **Bonus** Cindy had 7 storybooks, and Mark had twice as many. Cindy got 6 more storybooks for her birthday. Who has the most storybooks now? |

# Lesson └-10    Solving Problems by Drawing Pictures

PURPOSES
- To draw a picture about each problem.

- To use the picture to solve the problem.

- To state how the picture helps to solve the problem.

- To follow the steps of the major problem-solving approach to solve the problems.

## DIRECTIONS

**1. Sample Problem**

Give the children a copy of the student problem page and read the following problem slowly to them:

> I have 9 marbles.
>
> You have 12 marbles.
>
> How many marbles do we have together?

**2. Major Problem-Solving Approach**

Discuss the problem with the children as follows:

*Marbles.*

1   What is the problem about?

*How many marbles do we have together?*

2   What is the question?

*I have 9 marbles, and you have 12 marbles.*

3   What do you need to know to solve the problem?

*2 groups.*

4   Let's look at the picture about the problem. How many groups of marbles are there?

*9 and 12*

How many marbles are there in each group?

*Add the number of marbles I have to the number of marbles you have.*

5   How will you solve the problem? What will you do to solve the problem?

*I will count the number of marbles together.*

6   How will you use the picture to solve the problem?

*Because the picture shows
the 9 marbles I have
and the 12 marbles you have.*

Why?

7  What do you think your answer will be? Will it be greater than 12?

*9 + 12 =* _____

8  Write a number sentence for this problem.

9  Compute your answer.

10  What did you guess your answer would be? Is it the same?

*We have 21 marbles together.*

11  Give your answer in a sentence.

Follow a similar procedure with the problems for Lesson L-10 on the next page. With each problem, however, encourage the children to draw their own pictures of the problem and to use their pictures to solve the problem.

**ANSWERS**
**(For Student Problems)**

1  There are 17 apples altogether.

2  There are 22 umbrellas altogether.

3  16 slices of cake are left.

4  Tom is 14 years old.

5  Frank used 16 slices of bread.

*Bonus*  The children have 28 cards altogether.

**SAMPLE PROBLEM**

I have 9 marbles. You have 12
marbles. How many marbles do we
have altogether?

| | |
|---|---|
| 1  There are 8 green apples and 9 red apples in the basket. How many apples are there altogether? | 2  There are 15 black umbrellas and 7 blue umbrellas in the store. How many umbrellas are there altogether? |
| 3  There are 20 slices of cake on the table. Mary ate 4 slices. How many slices of cake are left? | 4  It is Tom's birthday. His mother has 8 candles for his cake. She needs 6 more. How old is Tom? |
| 5  Frank made 8 peanut butter and jelly sandwiches for the school picnic. He used 2 slices of bread for each sandwich. How many slices of bread did Frank use? | *Bonus*  Brian, Terry, and Robin are playing cards. Brian has 11 cards, Terry has 5 cards, and Robin has 12 cards. How many cards do they have altogether? |

# Lesson ∟-11  Solving Problems from Related Diagrams

PURPOSES

- To use diagrams when solving problems.

- To state how each diagram helps to solve a particular problem.

- To follow the steps of the major problem-solving approach to solve the problems.

DIRECTIONS

**1. Introduction and Discussion**

Give each child a copy of the diagrams for Lesson ∟-11 (see Diagrams to accompany Lesson ∟-11). Then tell the children to look at the top of their diagram sheet where they can see two groups of straight lines and ask them:

*2*    1  How many groups of straight lines are there?

*8*    2  How many straight lines are in the first group?

*8*    3  How many straight lines are in the second group?

**2. Sample Problem**

Read the following problem slowly to the children:

Paula and Andy have 8 crayons each.

How many crayons do they have together?

**3. Major Problem-Solving Approach**

Discuss the problem with the children by asking them the following questions:

*Crayons.*    1  What is the problem about?

*How many crayons do Paula and Andy have together?*    2  What is the question? What do you want to find out to solve the problem?

*Paula and Andy have 8 crayons each.*    3  What do you need to know to solve the problem?

*Add the number of crayons Paula has to the number of crayons Andy has; or multiply the number of crayons each has by 2.*

4 How will you solve the problem? What will you do to solve the problem?

*Each straight line represents a crayon. The first group of 8 straight lines represents the number of crayons Paula has, and the second group of 8 straight lines represents the number of crayons Andy has. If I count all of the straight lines in the diagram together, I will find the answer.*

5 How could you use the diagram to find your answer?

$$8 + 8 = \underline{\hspace{1cm}} \text{ or}$$
$$2 \times 8 = \underline{\hspace{1cm}}$$

6 Write a number sentence for this problem.

7 What do you think your answer will be? Will it be greater or less than 8?

8 Find your answer using the diagram.

9 What did you think your answer would be? Is it the same?

*Paula and Andy have 16 crayons together.*

10 How many crayons do Paula and Andy have together? Give your answer in a sentence.

Continue this procedure with the student problems for Lesson L-11 and the accompanying diagrams. (The children do not need to receive copies of the student problem page; however, this is at the option of the classroom teacher.) You may want to do one or two more together and then just read the remaining problems to the children, letting them do the last few on their own. Encourage the children to use the diagrams to help them to solve the problems.

**ANSWERS**
**(For Student Problems)**

1 Anne has 15 pennies now.

2 8 people will have to stand.

3 There are 24 trees in all.

4 The children ate 18 cookies in all.

5 Farmer Brown's hen laid 18 eggs in all.

*Bonus* John ran 28 miles altogether.

**LESSON L-11**

**SAMPLE PROBLEM**

Paula and Andy have 8 crayons each.

How many crayons do they have

altogether?

| | |
|---|---|
| 1 Anne has 9 pennies. Her father gave her 6 more. How many pennies does Anne have now? | 2 There are only 5 chairs in the doctor's waiting room. 13 people are waiting. How many people will have to stand? |
| 3 There are 8 oak trees and 16 pine trees growing in the park. How many trees are there in all? | 4 Sally ate 6 cookies, John ate 9 cookies, and Amy ate 3 cookies. How many cookies did they eat in all? |
| 5 Farmer Brown's hen laid 5 eggs on Monday, 6 eggs on Tuesday, and 7 eggs on Wednesday. How many eggs did Farmer Brown's hen lay in all? (Draw circles to show the eggs.) | *Bonus* John ran 4 miles every day for a week. How many miles did he run altogether? (Make your own diagram to show how this problem can be solved.) |

Name_____

Sample

---

1.

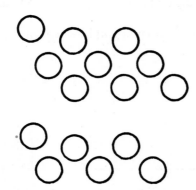

2.

$\underline{|} \quad \underline{|} \quad \underline{|} \quad \underline{|} \quad \underline{|}$

$|\quad|\quad|\quad|\quad|$

$|\quad|\quad|$

---

3.

Y Y Y Y Y Y Y

Y Y Y Y Y Y Y Y
Y Y Y Y Y Y Y Y

4.

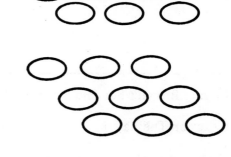

# Lesson ∟-12 Solving Problems by Drawing Diagrams

**PURPOSES**
- To help the children draw a simple diagram about each problem and to use their diagram to solve the problem.

- To review the major problem-solving approach.

**DIRECTIONS**

**1. Sample Problem**

Read the following problem slowly to the children:

> Robin bought 3 packs of candy.
>
> There are 6 candies in each pack.
>
> How many candies did Robin buy altogether?

**2. Major Problem-Solving Approach**

Discuss the problem with the children by asking them the following questions:

*Candies.*

1   What is the problem about?

*How many candies did Robin buy altogether?*

2   What is the question?

*Robin bought 3 packs of candies, and there were 6 candies in each pack.*

3   What do you need to know to solve the problem?

4   Instead of drawing a picture about the problem, this time we will draw a diagram. Let a circle (○) represent a candy and a straight line (_____) the pack.

*6*     How many circles will we draw for the first pack of candies?

*6*     How many circles will we draw for the second pack of candies?

*6*     How many circles will we draw for the third pack of candies?

*3*     How many groups of 6 circles do we have?

     Draw a line under each group of 6 candies.

*3*     How many straight lines do we have?

*3*     How many packs of candies do we have?

| ○○○○○○ | ○○○○○○ | ○○○○○○ |
|---|---|---|
| 6 candies | 6 candies | 6 candies |
| 1 pack | 1 pack | 1 pack |

*Add the number of candies in a pack together 3 times; or multiply the number of candies in each pack by the number of packs Robin bought.*

5 How will you solve the problem? What will you do to solve the problem?

*Add the number of circles together.*

*Because there are 3 groups of 6 circles representing the 3 packs of 6 candies.*

*6 + 6 + 6 = _____ or*
*3 × 6 = _____*

6 How will you use your diagram to solve the problem?

Why?

7 Write a number sentence for this problem.

8 What do you think your answer will be? Will it be greater or less than 20?

9 Find your answer using your diagram.

10 What did you guess your answer would be? Is it the same?

*Robin bought 18 candies altogether.*

11 Give your answer in a sentence.

Follow a similar procedure for the remaining problems for Lesson L-12. (The children do not need to receive a copy of the student problem page; however, this is at the option of the classroom teacher.) You may want to do one or two more together to give the children practice at drawing a diagram of a problem situation. Encourage the children to use the diagrams they have drawn to help them to solve the problem.

**ANSWERS**
**(For Student Problems)**

1 Lucy has read 22 pages.

2 Jack has 16 pages left to read.

3 The girls counted 24 buttons on their raincoats altogether.

4 Adam used 28 slices of bread altogether.

5 Tom and Sally were 17 meters apart.

*Bonus* Each girl got 2 candies. There was 1 candy left over.

**LESSON L-12**

Name_____

**SAMPLE PROBLEM**

Robin bought 3 packs of candies.

There are 6 candies in each pack.

How many candies did Robin buy

altogether?

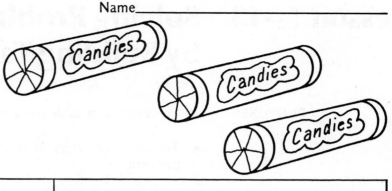

| | |
|---|---|
| 1  Lucy is reading *Charlotte's Web*. She has read 2 chapters already. There are 10 pages in the first chapter and 12 pages in the second chapter. How many pages has Lucy read? | 2  Jack is reading *The Plant Sitter* to his little sister. There are 25 pages in the book altogether. Jack has read 9 already. How many more pages does he still need to read? |
| 3  Sally has 8 buttons on her raincoat, Lisa has 9 buttons, and May has 7 buttons. They decided to count the number of buttons they have on their raincoats altogether. What answer did they get? | 4  Adam fed the ducks in the park 4 slices of bread every day for a week. How many slices of bread did he use to feed the ducks altogether? |
| 5  Tom and Sally ran in opposite directions, starting from the same point. Tom ran 8 meters, and Sally ran 9 meters. How far away from each other were they then? | *Bonus*  15 candies were divided equally among 7 girls. How many candies did each girl get? How many candies were left over? |

# Lesson L-13　Solving Problems by Building Tables

PURPOSES

- To construct a table for each problem and to use it to solve the problem.

- To follow the steps of the major problem-solving approach to solve the problem.

**DIRECTIONS**

**1. Sample Problem**

Read the following problem slowly to the children:

> Tom has 2 more brothers than John has.
>
> How many brothers does Tom have?

**2. Major Problem-Solving Approach**

Discuss the problem with the children as follows:

*Brothers.*

1　What is the problem about?

*How many brothers does Tom have?*

2　What is the question?

*How many brothers John has and that Tom has 2 more brothers than John.*

3　What do you need to know to solve the problem?

*I will add 2 to the number of brothers John has.*

4　How will you solve the problem? What will you do to solve the problem?

*No.*

5　Do you know the number of brothers John has?

*Tom would have 2 brothers.*

*Because Tom has 2 more brothers than John and $0 + 2 = 2$.*

6　If John had no brothers, how many brothers would Tom have? Why?

*Tom would have 3 brothers because $2 + 1 = 3$.*

7　If John had 1 brother, how many brothers would Tom have?

*Tom would have 4 brothers because $2 + 2 = 4$.*

8　If John had 2 brothers, how many brothers would Tom have?

9　We can write our answer to this problem in the form of a table. Write this table on the blackboard with help from the children.

| Number of Brothers John Has | Number of Brothers Tom Has |
|---|---|
| 0 | 2 |
| 1 | 3 |
| 2 | 4 |
| 3 | 5 |
| 4 | 6 |
| 5 | 7 |

10  We can state our answer sentences as follows:

If John has no brothers, Tom has 2 brothers.

If John has 1 brother, Tom has 3 brothers.

If John has 2 brothers, Tom has 4 brothers.

If John has 3 brothers, Tom has 5 brothers.

If John has 4 brothers, Tom has 6 brothers.

If John has 5 brothers, Tom has 7 brothers.

Tom has between 2 and 7 brothers, since it is unlikely that John has more than 5 brothers.

Follow a similar procedure with the student problems at the end of this lesson. (The children do not need to receive copies of the student problem page; however, this is at the option of the classroom teacher.) Construct a table for each problem. You may wish to do another problem with the children to give them practice at constructing a table. The length of the table for each of the remaining problems is stipulated.

**ANSWERS AND TABLES (For Student Problems)**

*Number of Toy Cars*

1
| Joe | Andy |
|---|---|
| 9 | 12 |
| 10 | 13 |
| 11 | 14 |
| 12 | 15 |

Andy has between 12 and 15 toy cars.

*Number of Minutes*

2
| Joan | Sam |
|---|---|
| 5 | 10 |
| 6 | 11 |
| 7 | 12 |
| 8 | 13 |
| 9 | 14 |
| 10 | 15 |

It takes Sam between 10 and 15 minutes to walk to school.

### Number of Marbles

3    Robert                Susan

| Robert | Susan |
|--------|-------|
| 10 | 4 |
| 11 | 5 |
| 12 | 6 |
| 13 | 7 |
| 14 | 8 |
| 15 | 9 |

Susan has between 4 and 9 marbles.

### Number of Apples

4    Anne                Sue

| Anne | Sue |
|------|-----|
| 9 | 5 |
| 10 | 6 |
| 11 | 7 |
| 12 | 8 |
| 13 | 9 |

Sue picked between 5 and 9 apples.

### Number of Candies

5    Amy                Lyn

| Amy | Lyn |
|-----|-----|
| 7 | 3 |
| 8 | 4 |
| 9 | 5 |
| 10 | 6 |

Lyn ate between 3 and 6 candies.

### Weight in Kilograms

**Bonus**    John                Bill

| John | Bill |
|------|------|
| 30 | 33 |
| 31 | 34 |
| 32 | 35 |
| 33 | 36 |
| 34 | 37 |
| 35 | 38 |

Bill weighs between 33 and 38 kg.

**SAMPLE PROBLEM**

Tom has 2 more brothers than John

has. How many brothers does Tom

have?

| | |
|---|---|
| 1  Andy has 3 more toy cars than Joe has. Joe has between 9 and 12 toy cars. How many toy cars does Andy have? | 2  It takes Joan between 5 and 10 minutes to walk to school. It takes Sam 5 more minutes to walk to school than it takes Joan. How many minutes does it take Sam to walk to school? |
| 3  Robert has between 10 and 15 marbles. Susan has 6 fewer marbles than Robert has. How many marbles does Susan have? | 4  Anne picked between 9 and 13 apples. Sue picked 4 fewer apples than Anne. How many apples did Sue pick? |
| 5  Lyn ate 4 fewer candies than Amy. Amy ate at least 7 but not more than 10. How many candies could Lyn have eaten? | *Bonus*  John weighs between 30 kg and 35 kg. Bill weighs 3 kg more than John. How many kg does Bill weigh? |

# Lesson L-14   Solving Problems from a Graph

PURPOSES
- To solve problems using a graph.

- To develop the children's ability to discriminate.

- To review the major problem-solving approach.

DIRECTIONS

1. Introduction

Give each child a copy of the birthday block graph (see Graph for Lesson L-14) and discuss it with them. How many months are there in a year? What are they? Tell the children that each block represents a child who has a birthday in a certain month. In January, only one child has a birthday. In February, two children have birthdays.

2. Discussion

Ask the children questions about the graph to give them practice at reading from it.

1   How many children have birthdays in March, April, May, . . . ?

2   Which month has the most birthdays?

3   How many birthdays does _____ have?

4   Which month has no birthdays?

5   How many months have 2 birthdays?

3. Sample Problem

Read the following problem slowly to the children:

How many children have birthdays in February and March?

4. Major Problem-Solving Approach

*Birthdays.*

Discuss the problem with the children by asking them the following questions:

1   What is the problem about?

*How many children have birthdays in February and March?*

2  What is the question?

*The number of children who have a birthday in February and the number of children who have a birthday in March.*

3  What do you need to know to solve the problem?

*I will add the number of children who have a birthday in February to the number of children who have a birthday in March.*

4  How will you solve the problem? What will you do to solve the problem?

*By looking at the graph and counting the number of blocks above February.*

5  How will you find out the number of children who have a birthday in February?

*2*

How many blocks did you count?

*By looking at the graph and counting the number of blocks above March.*

6  How will you find out the number of children who have a birthday in March?

*7*

How many blocks did you count?

$2 + 7 = $ _____

7  Write a number sentence for this problem.

8  What do you think your answer will be?

9  Find your answer using the graph.

10  What did you guess your answer would be? Is it the same?

*9 children have birthdays in February and March.*

11  Give your answer in a sentence.

Follow a similar procedure for the problems on the student problem page. (The children do not need to receive a copy of the student problem page for Lesson ∟-14; however, this is at the option of the classroom teacher.) You may want to do another problem together to give the children practice at reading and using information from the graph. Then read the remaining problems to the children and let them find the solutions on their own. Encourage them to use the graph to find their answers.

**ANSWERS**
**(For Student Problems)**

1  9 children have birthdays in September and October.

2  3 more children have birthdays in October than in June.

**3** 4 more children have birthdays in March than in May.

**4** 14 children have birthdays in March, May, and September.

**5** 10 children have birthdays in January, February, and March.

*Bonus* 5 months have only two birthdays. 10 children have birthdays in these months.

Name_____

**SAMPLE PROBLEM**

How many children have birthdays in February and March?

| | |
|---|---|
| 1   How many children have birthdays in September and October? | 2   How many more children have birthdays in October than in June? |
| 3   How many more children have birthdays in March than in May? | 4   How many children have birthdays in March, May, and September? |
| 5   How many children have birthdays in January, February, and March? | *Bonus*   How many months have only two birthdays? How many children have birthdays in these months? |

Name_____

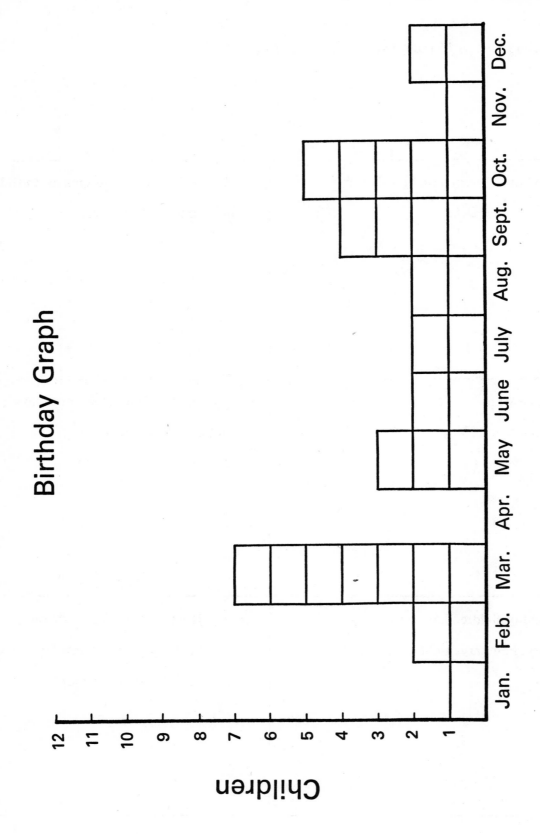

Birthday Graph

# Lesson ∟-15 Solving Two-Step Problems with Pictures

**PURPOSES**

- To review the major problem-solving approach by presenting two-step word problems.

- For the children to use pictures to help solve the problems.

**DIRECTIONS**

**1. Sample Problem**

Give each child a copy of the Pictures for Lesson ∟-15 and ask them to look at the kites. Read the following problem to them:

> Jane has 4 kites.
>
> Ellen has twice as many.
>
> How many kites do they have altogether?

**2. Major Problem-Solving Approach**

Discuss the problem with the children by asking them the following questions:

*Kites.*

1 What is the problem about?

*How many kites do Jane and Ellen have altogether?*

2 What is the question?

3 Look at the picture.

*3*

How many groups of kites are there?

*4*

How many kites are in each group?

The first group shows the 4 kites Jane has.

The other two groups show the kites Ellen has.

*Jane has 4 kites, and Ellen has twice as many.*

4 What do you need to know to solve the problem?

*I will multiply the number of kites Jane has by 2 to get Ellen's total and then add the number of kites Jane has to my answer; or I will add the number of kites Jane has together 3 times; or I will count Ellen's kites and add them to the 4 that Jane has.*

5 How will you solve the problem? What will you do to solve the problem?

$2 \times 4 = \underline{\hspace{1.5cm}}$
$+ 4 = \underline{\hspace{1.5cm}}$ *or*
$4 + 4 + 4 = \underline{\hspace{1.5cm}}$
*or* $8 + 4 = \underline{\hspace{1.5cm}}$

*I will count all the kites in the picture.*

*Because the picture shows the number of kites Jane has and the number of kites Ellen has.*

*Jane and Ellen have 12 kites altogether.*

6  Write a number sentence for this problem.

7  How could you use your picture to find the answer to the problem?

   Why?

8  What do you think your answer will be? Will it be greater or less than 8?

9  Find your answer and complete the number sentence.

10  What did you guess your answer would be? Is it the same?

11  Give your answer in a sentence.

You may wish to do one or two more problems from Lesson L-15 together and then read the remaining ones to the children, letting them do the last few on their own. (The children do not need to receive copies of the student problem page for Lesson L-15; however, this is at the option of the classroom teacher.) Encourage them to use the pictures to solve the problems.

**ANSWERS**
**(For Student Problems)**

1  Tom has 7 apples left.

2  Frances has $10 left.

3  John has 15 grapes left.

4  Mrs. Brown has 18 sheep now.

5  Dave has 18 colored pencils now.

*Bonus*  Frank and Joe have 28 marbles altogether.

# LESSON L-15

Name_____

**SAMPLE PROBLEM**

Jane has 4 kites. Ellen has twice as many. How many kites do they have altogether?

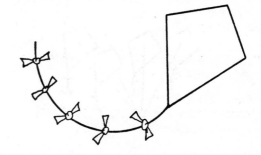

| | |
|---|---|
| 1  Tom has 16 apples. He ate half of them and gave 1 to Maureen. How many apples does Tom have left? | 2  Frances had $20. She bought 2 umbrellas for $5 each. How much money does Frances have left? |
| 3  John had 2 bunches of grapes. There were 9 grapes on each bunch. He ate 3 grapes. How many grapes does John have left? | 4  Mrs. Brown has 20 sheep. 3 sheep got lost. Mrs. Brown only found 1 of them. How many sheep does Mrs. Brown have now? |
| 5  Dave had 12 colored pencils. He lost half of them, so he bought 12 more. How many colored pencils does Dave have now? | *Bonus*  Frank has 7 marbles. Joe has 3 times as many marbles. How many marbles do they have altogether? |

　　　　Name_____

**1.**

**2.**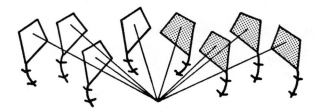

**3.**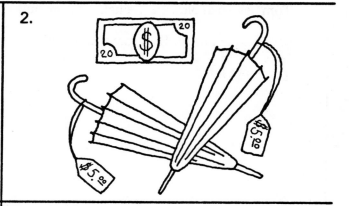

**4.**

**5.**

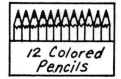

12 Colored Pencils

**Bonus:**

# Lesson L-16 Writing and Solving Our Own Problems

PURPOSES
- For the children to make up and write their own problems about the following:

  7 chocolate chip cookies and 9 peanut butter cookies;

  15 green apples and 8 red apples;

  2 white mice and 6 brown mice.

- For the children to base their problems on the following types of number sentences: $7 + 9 =$ _____ ; $15 - 8 =$ _____ ; $6 + 2 =$ _____ .

- For the children to follow the steps of the major problem-solving approach to solve their own problems.

DIRECTIONS

**1. Introduction and Discussion**

*Cookies.*

*There are 7 chocolate chip cookies and 9 peanut butter cookies.*

*How many cookies are there altogether?; How many cookies did Joe eat?; etc.*

Ask the children to make up a problem about 7 chocolate chip cookies and 9 peanut butter cookies. Encourage them by asking the following questions:

1  What will the problem be about?

2  What will the important facts in our problem be?

3  What will our question be?

**2. Sample Problem**

Write one of the problems on the blackboard that the children made up.

> Joe ate 7 chocolate chip cookies and 9 peanut butter cookies. How many cookies did Joe eat altogether?

Have the children copy the problem on their worksheets.

**3. Major Problem-Solving Approach**

Solve the problem following the steps of the major problem-solving approach. (The steps for this procedure are outlined in detail in Chapter 1.)

Continue this procedure with the number sentence 7 + 9 = _____ from Problem 1 on the student problem page. This time, however, get the children to use their own ideas to make up what the problem is about. Help the children to write their problems; and if they have any difficulty in solving them, use the steps of the major problem-solving approach to work through the tough spots. Problems 2 and 3 and Problems 4 and 5 are arranged in pairs that can complement each other. In the first problem of each pair, the children are given the main idea and important facts but not the question; in the second instance, the children are given part of the important facts, but they have to supply the rest of the information themselves.

**ANSWERS**
**(For Student Problems)**

The answers will vary depending on the problems devised by each student. Have the children check each other's work to see that problems make sense and answers are correct.

Name_____

**SAMPLE PROBLEM**

Make up and write a problem about

7 chocolate chip cookies and 9 peanut

butter cookies.

| | |
|---|---|
| 1   $7 + 9 =$ _____ | 2   Make up and write a problem about 15 green apples and 8 red apples. |
| 3   $15 - 8 =$ _____ | 4   Make up and write a problem about 2 white mice and 6 brown mice. |
| 5   $6 + 2 =$ _____ | *Bonus*   Make up and write a problem about something you like. |

# Chapter 5

# GRADE 3 PROBLEM-SOLVING LESSONS
## (LEVEL ⊔)

The lessons and problems in this chapter are designed to meet the needs and capabilities of third-grade children. Although the problems posed are more complex and abstract than those in the previous chapters, they should not present any particular difficulties—provided that the children have already developed the needed prerequisite skills. To aid in this process, the major problem-solving approach is introduced in the first two lessons and developed throughout the series. The supporting techniques (using pictures, diagrams, tables, etc.) are also designed to help the children solve more difficult problems.

Each lesson begins with plans for the teacher, including questions and suggested responses for a sample problem; then a copy of the student page follows immediately. This arrangement provides the teacher with immediate access to the Purposes, Directions, and Answers for the lesson as well as a copy of the student page. Any student problem pages or supplemental problem-solving aids (such as pictures and charts) may be duplicated in quantities necessary for the teacher's own classroom use.

Although the lessons have been designed primarily to develop problem-solving skills, they also provide computation practice appropriate for children working at the third-grade level. Problems 1 and 2 for each lesson provide easy computations, while Problems 3, 4, and 5 are more difficult. The bonus problem might be completed only by the more advanced students. In addition, the lessons are sequenced such that a student who is not working up to grade level may be exposed to the same problem-solving approach and techniques, but with easier problems, by being assigned the Grade 2 (Level ⌐) problems, and one who is able to do advanced work could be assigned to problems from Grade 4 (Level □).*

---

*The Grade 4 lessons are from the companion book, *Math Problem Solving for Grades 4 through 8*, which is available from Allyn and Bacon, Inc., 7 Wells Avenue, Newton, MA 02159.

# Lesson ⊔-1  Introducing the Major Problem-Solving Approach

**PURPOSE**

- To introduce the children to the initial steps of the major problem-solving approach by:

  1  Finding the main idea in a problem.

  2  Determining what is wanted.

  3  Finding the important facts in a problem.

**DIRECTIONS**

**1. Sample Problem**

Read the following sample problem slowly with the children:

> Michael is putting 2 sandwiches in each lunch box.
>
> There are 4 lunch boxes.
>
> How many sandwiches will Michael need?

**2. Major Problem-Solving Approach**

Discuss the problem with the children by asking them the following questions:

*Sandwiches.*

1  What is the problem about?

*How many sandwiches will Michael need?*

2  What is the question? What do you need to find out to solve the problem?

*There are 4 lunch boxes, and Michael is putting 2 sandwiches in each lunch box.*

3  What do you need to know to solve the problem?

Follow a similar procedure with the problems for Lesson ⊔-1 at the end of the lesson. You may want to do one or two more together and then let the children do the last few problems on their own. It is not necessary for the students to solve the problems in this lesson; however, if they wish to do so, it is permissible. Discuss the problems orally when finished.

**OPTIONAL ANSWERS**
**(For Student Problems)**

*Sample*   Michael will need 8 sandwiches.

1   May sold 21 newspapers altogether.

2   There are 9 books left.

3   John can ride 33 miles in 3 days.

4   Cindy still has 7 kittens.

5   There are 28 children in Mr. Brown's class.

*Bonus*   Father will make 48 sandwiches in 3 weeks.

**LESSON ⊔-1**

Name_____

**SAMPLE PROBLEM**

Michael is putting 2 sandwiches in each lunch box. There are 4 lunch boxes. How many sandwiches will Michael need?

| | |
|---|---|
| 1   May sold 12 newspapers on Monday and 9 newspapers on Tuesday. How many did she sell altogether? | 2   There were 17 books on the shelf. 8 books were given away. How many are left? |
| 3   If John can ride 11 miles in one day, how many miles can he ride in 3 days? | 4   Cindy has 12 kittens. She gave 2 to her friend, and then she gave away 3 more. How many kittens does she have left? |
| 5   Mr. Brown's class is divided up into 4 teams. There are 7 children on each team. How many children are in Mr. Brown's class? | *Bonus*   Father makes 16 sandwiches each week for the family's lunches. How many sandwiches will he make in 3 weeks? |

# Lesson ⊔-2　Using the Major Problem-Solving Approach

PURPOSE

- To review and expand the steps of the major problem-solving approach by:

  1　Finding the main idea in the problem.

  2　Determining what is wanted, i.e., the question.

  3　Determining the important facts in the problem.

  4　Stating how to solve the problem.*

  5　Writing a number sentence for the problem.*

  6　Estimating the answer.*

  7　Computing the answer.*

  8　Comparing the answer with the estimation.*

  9　Stating the answer sentence.*

## DIRECTIONS

### 1. Sample Problem

Read the following sample problem slowly with the children:

> You had 30¢.
>
> You bought a pencil for 15¢.
>
> How much money do you have left?

### 2. Major Problem-Solving Approach

Lead the children to a solution of the sample problem using the following types of questions.

*Note: At this stage it is important that the children use each step when working through problems with you. When working on their own, they may leave out steps, but they should know what the steps are so that they can refer back if they have difficulty.*

---

*Steps 4 through 9 are being introduced for the first time. The students may now use all steps to solve any word problem.

| | |
|---|---|
| *Buying a pencil.* | 1 What is the problem about? |
| *How much money was left after I bought the pencil?* | 2 What is the question? What do you want to find out to solve the problem? |
| *I had 30¢, and I spent 15¢ for the pencil.* | 3 What do you need to know to solve the problem (i.e., the important facts)? |
| *Take the price of a pencil away from the amount of money I had.* | 4 Tell in your own words what you need to do to solve the problem. |
| *30¢ − 15¢ = _____* | 5 Write a number sentence for this problem. |
| | 6 What do you think your answer will be? |
| *30¢ − 15¢ = 15¢* | 7 Complete your number sentence. What is your answer? |
| | 8 What did you guess your answer would be? Is it the same? |
| *I have 15¢ left.* | 9 Give your answer in a sentence. |

Follow a similar procedure with the problems for Lesson ⊔-2 on the next page. You may want to do one or two more together to give the children practice at using the steps. Then only read the problems with the children, and let them do the last few problems on their own. Discuss the problems orally when finished.

### ANSWERS
### (For Student Problems)

1 There are 25 children in the classroom.

2 We traveled 27 miles altogether.

3 The theater has 60 seats.

4 The girls have 18 balloons altogether.

5 86 children went to the circus on Friday and Saturday.

*Bonus* John and Christy have 32 marbles altogether.

**LESSON ⊔-2**                                    Name_____

**SAMPLE PROBLEM**

You had 30¢. You bought a pencil for
15¢. How much money do you have
left?

---

| | |
|---|---|
| 1   There are 13 girls and 12 boys in the classroom. How many children are in the classroom altogether? | 2   On a school trip we traveled 12 miles on Friday, 6 miles on Saturday, and 9 miles on Sunday. How many miles did we travel in all? |
| 3   A theater has 6 rows of 10 seats. How many seats does the theater have? | 4   6 girls are playing. Each girl has 3 balloons. How many balloons do they have altogether? |
| 5   52 children went to the circus on Friday. 34 children went on Saturday. How many children went to the circus on those 2 days? | *Bonus*   John has 15 marbles. Christy has 2 more marbles than John. How many marbles do they have together? |

# Lesson ⊔-3   Using Mathematical Vocabulary

PURPOSES

- To instruct the children in how to solve problems containing the following vocabulary: *twice, equals, half, greatest,* and *least.*

- To provide the children with further instruction in the steps of the major problem-solving approach.

DIRECTIONS

**1. Sample Problem**

Read the following sample problem slowly with the children:

> Sue buys 4 apples *twice* a week.
>
> How many apples does she buy each week?

**2. Major Problem-Solving Approach**

Discuss the problem with the children by asking them the following questions:

*Apples.*

1   What is the problem about?

*How many apples does Sue buy each week?*

2   What is the question?

*Sue buys 4 apples twice a week.*

3   What do you need to know to solve the problem?

*I will add the number of apples Sue buys together twice; or I will multiply the number of apples Sue buys one time by 2.*

4   Tell in your own words how you would solve this problem.

*Twice.*

5   Which word in the problem tells you how to solve it?

*2 times.*

What does "twice" mean?

*Sue buys 4 apples 2 times a week. How many apples does she buy each week?*

Can you state the problem in another way without using the word "twice"?

*Addition or multiplication.*

6   What operation will you use?

$4 + 4 = \rule{1.5cm}{0.4pt}$ *or*
$2 \times 4 = \rule{1.5cm}{0.4pt}$

7   Write a number sentence for this problem.

8   What do you think your answer will be?

9 Add or multiply to solve your number sentence. What is your answer?

10 What did you guess your answer would be? Is it the same?

*Sue buys 8 apples each week.*

11 Give your answer in a sentence.

Follow a similar procedure with the student problems on the next page. You may want to do one or two more together to give the children practice at following the steps and to explain any of the mathematical terms that they are not already familiar with. You may also wish to have them underline the terms *twice, equals, half, greatest,* and *least.* Read all the problems with the children, but let them try to solve several of the problems by themselves. Discuss all of the problems with the children when they have finished.

**ANSWERS**
**(For Student Problems)**

1 The teacher must order 12 more spelling books.

2 Jill has 8 crayons.

3 The children would drink at least 15 cups of milk in 3 days.

4 10 people can sit down at the same time.

5 The girls have 21 dolls altogether.

*Bonus* Larry wanted 3 eggs for breakfast.

LESSON ⊔-3                                Name_____

**SAMPLE PROBLEM**

Sue buys 4 apples *twice* a week. How
many apples does she buy each week?

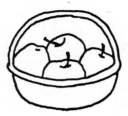

| | |
|---|---|
| 1  The teacher has 21 reading books and 9 spelling books. How many more spelling books must the teacher order so that the number of reading books equals the number of spelling books? | 2  Andy has 16 crayons. Jill has half as many crayons as Andy has. How many crayons does Jill have? |
| 3  There are 5 children in the classroom. If each child drinks 1 cup or more of milk a day, what is the least amount of milk they would drink in 3 days? | 4  There are 4 chairs and 2 benches in a room. If 3 people can sit on each bench, and 1 person can sit on each chair, what is the greatest number of people who can sit down at the same time? |
| 5  Anne has 6 dolls. Mary has twice as many dolls as Anne has. Cindy has half as many dolls as Anne has. How many dolls do the girls have altogether? | *Bonus*  Larry wanted fried eggs for breakfast. The egg carton was half full, but that was twice as many eggs as he wanted to eat. How many eggs did he wish to eat for breakfast? |

**189**

# Lesson ⎵-4  Finding Key Words and Phrases

PURPOSES

- To provide instruction in locating the following key words and phrases and relating them to their appropriate operations:

  "left" — subtraction
  "in all" — addition or multiplication
  "altogether" — addition or multiplication

- To further instruct children in the steps of the major problem-solving approach.


DIRECTIONS

**1. Sample Problem**

Read the following sample problem slowly with the children:

> Mary picked 12 oranges.
>
> Sara picked 8 oranges.
>
> How many oranges did they pick *altogether*?


**2. Major Problem-Solving Approach**

Discuss the problem with the children by asking them the following questions:

*Oranges.*

1  What is the problem about?

*How many oranges did Mary and Sara pick altogether?*

2  What is the question?

*Mary picked 12 oranges, and Sara picked 8 oranges.*

3  What do you need to know to solve the problem?

*Add the number of oranges Mary picked to the number of oranges Sara picked.*

4  Tell in your own words what you need to do to solve the problem.

*Altogether.*

Why will you add? Is there any word in the problem that lets you know you must add to find your answer?

*Because I am putting things together.*

Why?

*They picked 20 oranges altogether.*

5  Continue the process by asking the children to write a number sentence, estimate their answer, compare their estimation with their answer, and state their answer in a sentence.


190

Have the students locate, underline, and discuss the meanings of the key words *altogether*, *left*, and *in all* in Problems 1, 2, and 3 on the following page. Then have them complete the remaining problems for Lesson ⌴-4 in a similar fashion.

**ANSWERS**
**(For Student Problems)**

1  They have 22 marbles altogether.

2  Tom has 70¢ left.

3  There are 32 books in all.

4  Pat's mother baked 23 cakes altogether.

5  The boys caught 13 fish altogether.

*Bonus*  Jerry got back 82¢ in change.

**SAMPLE PROBLEM**

Mary picked 12 oranges. Sara picked

8 oranges. How many oranges did

they pick *altogether*?

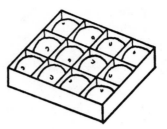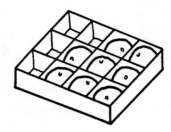

| | |
|---|---|
| 1   Amy has 9 marbles. Steve has 13 marbles. How many marbles do they have altogether? | 2   Tom had $1. He bought a box of crayons for 30¢. How much money does Tom have left? |
| 3   There are 8 books in each stack. There are 4 stacks. How many books are there in all? | 4   Pat's mother baked 4 small cakes in the morning, 12 small cakes in the afternoon, and 7 cakes at night. How many cakes did she bake altogether? |
| 5   6 boys went fishing. 5 boys caught 2 fish each, and 1 boy caught 3 fish. How many fish did they catch altogether? | *Bonus*   Jerry bought a tablet for 29¢, an eraser for 15¢, a pencil for 15¢, and a box of crayons for 59¢. How much change did he have left from $2? |

# Lesson ⊔-5   Problem Solving and Vocabulary Instruction

- To introduce the children to problems containing two different sets, both of which belong to a larger universal set:

  | parents and children | — | people |
  |---|---|---|
  | daffodils and tulips | — | flowers |
  | butterflies and bees | — | insects |
  | dogs, pups, and cats | — | pets |
  | cows, sheep, and pigs | — | farm animals |
  | canaries and parrots | — | birds |

- To continue the use of the major problem-solving approach.

## DIRECTIONS

**1. Introduction and Discussion**

Begin with a group discussion about how sets can relate to a universal set. For example, ask the following questions: Do you have any flowers growing in your garden? What flowers do you like the best? Does a daisy belong to the set of flowers? Does a leaf belong to the set of flowers? Why not?

**2. Sample Problem**

Read the following sample problem with the children:

> Kevin bought 9 daffodils and 9 tulips.
>
> How many flowers did he buy altogether?

**3. Major Problem-Solving Approach**

Discuss the problem with the children by asking them the following questions:

*Buying flowers.*

1  What is the problem about?

*How many flowers did Kevin buy?*

2  What is the question?

*Kevin bought 9 daffodils and 9 tulips.*

3  What do you need to know to solve the problem?

*I will add the number of daffodils Kevin bought to the number of tulips he bought.*

4  Tell in your own words what you need to do to solve the problem.

*Addition.*

$9 + 9 =$ _____

$9 + 9 = 18$

*Kevin bought 18 flowers altogether.*

5  What operation will you use?

6  Write a number sentence.

7  Estimate your answer.

8  Compute the answer.

9  Compare the estimation with the answer.

10  State the answer in a sentence.

Follow a similar procedure with the student problems for Lesson ⊔-5. If further discussion of sets and universal sets is necessary, use the examples noted with the purposes above.

## ANSWERS
### (For Student Problems)

1  The boys have 8 birds altogether.

2  Sue has 11 pets.

3  Dennis has 7 insects left.

4  Mr. Jones has 24 farm animals.

5  There are 25 people at the party.

*Bonus*  Wendy had 7 cats before giving any away.

Name_____

**SAMPLE PROBLEM**

Kevin bought 9 daffodils and 9 tulips.

How many flowers did he buy

altogether?

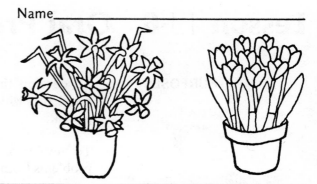

| | |
|---|---|
| 1  John has 5 canaries and 1 parrot. Peter has 2 parrots. How many birds do the boys have altogether? | 2  Sue's dog Ginger had 9 pups. Sue also has a cat. How many pets does Sue have? |
| 3  Dennis is collecting insects. He caught 5 butterflies and 3 bees. One of the butterflies got away. How many insects does he have left? | 4  Mr. Jones has 10 cows, 6 sheep, 8 pigs, and 1 tractor. How many farm animals does Mr. Jones have? |
| 5  10 children are having a party. 5 of the children have both of their parents at the party. The rest of the children have 1 parent at the party. How many people are at the party? | *Bonus*  Wendy gave 2 kittens away to a neighbor and 3 kittens away to friends. She kept 1 kitten and the mother cat. How many cats did she have before giving any away? |

# Lesson ⊔-6  Oral Presentation of Problems

- To develop the children's listening skills by reading to them simple oral problems, which they will solve mentally without the use of paper and pencil.

- To review the major problem-solving approach when presenting oral problems to the children.

## DIRECTIONS

**1. Sample Problem**

Tell the children that you are going to read a problem to them, and you want them to tell you what the problem is about and what question they will need to answer:

> A box of apples costs $3.
>
> How much will 4 boxes cost?

**2. Major Problem-Solving Approach**

After the first reading, ask:

*The cost of apples.*

1  What is the problem about?

*How much will 4 boxes of apples cost?*

2  What is the question?

**3. Continue the Major Problem-Solving Approach**

Reread the problem once again and ask the children:

*The price of one box of apples and how many boxes there are.*

3  What do you need to know to solve the problem?

*Multiply the number of boxes by the price of one box; or add the price of a box of apples together 4 times because there are 4 boxes of apples.*

4  Tell in your own words what you need to do to solve the problem.

5  Do this multiplication/addition in your head.

6 Write only your answer on your paper.

*4 boxes of apples cost $12.*

7 Give your answer in a sentence.

Tell the children that you are going to read five or six more problems to them. (The students do not need to receive copies of the student page for Lesson ⊔-6; however, this is at the option of the classroom teacher.) The first time the problem is read, they should listen to find out what the problem is about and what the question is. The second time, they should listen carefully for the important facts they need to know to solve the problem, decide how they will solve the problem, and think out the answer in their heads. They should write only the answers on their papers.

**ANSWERS**
**(For Student Problems)**

1 Candy watched television for 12 hours.

2 Maria spent $21 for the dress and skirt.

3 Robert was 11 miles from work.

4 Sam got 16 words correct.

5 Each girl will get 3 cookies.

*Bonus* Matt caught 7 fish.

**SAMPLE PROBLEM**

A box of apples cost $3. How much

will 4 boxes cost?

| | |
|---|---|
| 1  Candy watched television for 3 hours each day on Monday, Tuesday, Wednesday, and Thursday. How many hours did she watch television in those 4 days? | 2  Maria bought a dress for $9 and a skirt for $12. How much did she spend for them? |
| 3  Robert drives 19 miles to work each day. One day he had a flat tire after driving 8 miles. How far was he from work? | 4  Sam had 20 words on his spelling test. He missed 4. How many did he get correct? |
| 5  Kim and Sherry are baking cookies for a party. Kim baked 8 cookies, and Sherry baked 7 cookies. If 5 girls are at the party, how many cookies will each girl get? | *Bonus*  Andy, James, and Matt went fishing, and they caught 22 fish. Andy caught 8 fish, and Matt and James caught the same amount of fish. How many fish did Matt catch? |

# Lesson ⊔-7   Swimming Problems Presented Orally

<table>
<tr><td>PURPOSES</td><td>

• To develop the children's listening skills by reading to them simple oral problems, which they will solve mentally without the use of paper and pencil.

• To review the major problem-solving approach when presenting oral problems based on a theme.

• To provide the children with instructions in chart reading (see Chart for Lesson ⊔-7 on the following page).

</td></tr>
</table>

## DIRECTIONS

**1. Introduction and Discussion**

Show the children the swimming sign (Chart for Lesson ⊔-7 at the end of the lesson) and discuss it with them. How many children are there? What are their names? How old are they? How much will it cost John to go for a swim? How much will it cost _____ to go for a swim? Who will be charged the most? Who will be charged the least? How much would it cost you to go for a swim?

**2. Sample Problem**

Read the following problem twice to the children:

John had $1.

He went for a swim.

How much money does John have left?

**3. Major Problem-Solving Approach**

After the first reading, ask:

*John going for a swim.*

1   What is the problem about?

*How much money did John have left after he went for a swim?*

2   What is the question?

**4. Continue the Major Problem-Solving Approach**

Reread the problem again and ask the children to listen for the important facts necessary to solve the problem:

*How much money John had in the beginning and how much he paid to get into the swimming pool.*

3 What do you need to know to solve the problem?

*Subtract the price of a swim from the amount of money John had in the beginning.*

4 Tell in your own words what you need to do to solve the problem.

*50¢*

5 What price will John have to pay for a swim?

6 Do your subtraction in your head without writing anything on your paper.

7 Write only the answer on your paper.

*John has 50¢ left.*

8 Give your answer in a sentence.

Tell the children that you are going to read five more problems to them. The first time, they should listen to find out what the problem is about and what the question is. The second time, they should listen carefully for the important facts they need to know to solve the problem. Use the Swimming Price Chart to find out the admittance charges for the different children. Direct the children to decide how they will solve the problem and to think out the answer in their heads. Have them write only the answer on their papers.

ANSWERS
(For Student Problems)

1 Sue and Amy will need 50¢.

2 Tom and John will need 50¢ (no charge for Tom).

3 Sue will have 10¢ left.

4 John will have 50¢ left.

5 Amy has 25¢ left.

*Bonus* It cost John $2.00 to go swimming four days in a row.

Name_____

**SAMPLE PROBLEM** (See the Swimming Price Chart on the next page.)

John had $1. He went for a swim.

How much money does John have

left?

| | |
|---|---|
| 1  Sue and Amy are going swimming. Altogether, how much money will they need in order to get into the pool? | 2  Tom and John are going swimming. How much money will they need? |
| 3  Sue has 60¢. If she goes for a swim and takes Amy, how much money will she have left after paying for both of them? | 4  John has $1.50. He is going for a swim and taking Sue, Amy, and Tom. How much money will John have left? |
| 5  Amy had $1. She took a swim in the morning, and in the afternoon she took another swim and brought Sue. How much money does Amy have left? | *Bonus*  John went swimming 4 days in a row. How much did it cost him? |

Name_____

**City Swimming Pool**

| AGE | PRICE |
|---|---|
| Over 15 | 75¢ |
| 11–15 | 50¢ |
| 5–10 | 25¢ |
| Under 5 | Free |

Tom
4

Sue
9

Amy
6

John
12

# Lesson ⊔-8    Using Pictures To Help Solve Problems

PURPOSES
PURPOSES

- To review the major problem-solving approach by presenting problems to the children which are accompanied by pictures.

- To draw simple pictures or use manipulatives when solving problems.

DIRECTIONS

**1. Sample Problem**

Tell the children to look at the picture of 8 strawberries and 4 girls. (See the problems for Lesson ⊔-8.)

There are 8 strawberries and 4 girls.

How many strawberries will each girl get if they are divided equally among the 4 girls?

**2. Major Problem-Solving Approach**

Discuss the problem with the children by asking them the following questions:

*Strawberries.*

1  What is the problem about?

*How many strawberries will each girl get if the strawberries are divided equally among the girls?*

2  What is the question? What do you want to find out to solve the problem?

*8*

3  Discuss the picture with the children. How many strawberries are in the picture?

How are the strawberries arranged in the picture?

*They are divided into groups of 2.*

*4*

How many groups of 2 strawberries are there?

*4*

How many girls are there?

*There are 8 strawberries and 4 girls.*

4  What do you need to know to solve the problem?

*There are 8 strawberries in the picture divided into 4 groups of 2. There are 4 girls in the picture. Each girl can have 2 strawberries, since there are 4 groups of strawberries and 4 girls.*

5  How could you use the picture to find your answer?

*I will divide the number of strawberries by the number of girls; or I will subtract 4 strawberries from the total number of strawberries as many times as I can and count the number of times I subtracted to find my answer.*

$8 \div 4 =$ _____
or $8 - 4 =$ _____
$- 4 =$ _____

*Each girl will get 2 strawberries.*

*Note: When the children are working on their own, a student may wish to skip certain steps in the solution procedure – this is acceptable as long as the student understands the process.*

6  Tell in your own words how you would solve the problem.

7  Write a number sentence for this problem.

8  Give your answer in a sentence.

You may wish to select another of the student problems to work together in order that the children may practice using pictures when they have been provided and/or drawing their own in order to find their answer. Then let the children do the last few problems on their own.

### ANSWERS
### (For Student Problems)

1  Each child got 4 marbles.

2  The students made 18 posters altogether.

3  John has 5 cages.

4  Sally bought 24 buttons.

5  David made 6 sandwiches.

*Bonus*  Nancy spent $1.29 for the orange juice.

LESSON ⊔-8

**SAMPLE PROBLEM**

There are 8 strawberries and 4 girls.

How many strawberries will each girl

get if they are divided equally among

the 4 girls?

| | |
|---|---|
| 1   20 marbles were divided equally among 5 children. How many marbles did each child get? (Draw lines to the marbles each child will get.)       | 2   6 students made posters for the Spring Fair. They each made 3 posters. How many posters did they make altogether?     |
| 3   John has 15 white mice. He has 3 mice in each cage. How many cages does he have? (Draw the mice in their cages.) | 4   Sally is making a dress. She went to the store to buy some buttons. She bought 4 cards of buttons. There are 6 buttons on each card. How many buttons did Sally buy? (Draw a picture of the buttons.) |
| 5   David made sandwiches for lunch. He used 12 pieces of bread. How many sandwiches did he make? | *Bonus*   Nancy's mother sent her to the store to buy 3 cans of orange juice. Each can costs 43¢. How much did Nancy spend for the orange juice? |

# Lesson ⊔-9  Solving Problems by Drawing Pictures

**PURPOSES**

- To follow the steps of the major problem-solving approach.

- To draw a picture about each problem.

- To use the pictures to solve the problems.

- To state how the pictures help to solve the problems.

**DIRECTIONS**

**1. Sample Problem**

Read the following problem slowly to the children:

> Mrs. Jones had 12 eggs.
>
> She used 5 of them in a cake.
>
> How many eggs does she have left?

**2. Major Problem-Solving Approach**

Discuss the problem with the children by asking them the following questions:

*Using eggs to make a cake.*

1 What is the problem about?

*How many eggs does Mrs. Jones have left?*

2 What is the question? What do you want to find out to solve the problem?

*Mrs. Jones had 12 eggs, and she used 5 of them in a cake.*

3 What do you need to know to solve the problem?

4 Draw a picture about the problem.

*12 eggs.*

5 Describe what is in the picture. How many eggs were drawn? Why was the cake drawn?

*5 eggs.*

6 How many eggs were used in the cake?

*I will take the number of eggs Mrs. Jones used in the cake away from the number of eggs she had in the beginning.*

7 Tell in your own words what you need to do to solve the problem.

*12 eggs were drawn to show how many Mrs. Jones had in the beginning. She used 5 of them in a cake, so I will cross off 5 of them and count the number of eggs I have left; or I will draw an arrow from 5 of the eggs over to the cake and count the number of eggs that have no arrow leading to the cake.*

$$12 - 5 = \text{_____}$$

*Mrs. Jones has 7 eggs left.*

8  How will you use the picture to solve the problem?

9  Write a number sentence for this problem.

10  What do you think your answer will be?

11  Count the number of eggs that are left.

12  What did you guess your answer would be? Is it the same?

13  Give your answer in a sentence.

Follow a similar procedure for the student problems on the next page. You may want to do one or two more together to give the children practice at drawing a picture of the problem. Encourage the children to use the pictures they have drawn to help them to solve the problems.

**ANSWERS**
**(For Student Problems)**

1  Jane picked 15 oranges altogether.

2  Amy has 9 records.

3  Andy has 21 baseball cards.

4  Dana bought 15 marbles altogether.

5  There were 7 cokes left.

*Bonus*  Each person ate 2 hot dogs.

**LESSON ⊔-9**

**SAMPLE PROBLEM**

Mrs. Jones had 12 eggs. She used 5

of them in a cake. How many eggs

does she have left?

| | |
|---|---|
| 1   Jane picked 6 oranges on Monday and 9 oranges on Tuesday. How many oranges did she pick altogether? | 2   Amy has 5 fewer records than Paul. Paul has 14 records. How many records does Amy have? |
| 3   Andy has 3 piles of baseball cards. There are 7 cards in each pile. How many cards does he have? | 4   Dana bought 3 boxes of marbles. There are 5 marbles in each box. How many marbles did Dana buy altogether? |
| 5   Hannah bought 12 cokes to take home. Hannah drank 2 cokes, and her dad drank 3. How many cokes were left? | *Bonus*   There were 12 people at a picnic. They ate a total of 24 hot dogs. How many hot dogs did each person eat if each ate the same number of hot dogs? |

      

# Lesson ⊔-10   Using Diagrams To Solve Problems

PURPOSES

- To use diagrams when solving problems.

- To state how each diagram helps to solve a particular problem.

- To draw appropriate diagrams.

- To use the steps of the major problem-solving approach to solve each problem.

DIRECTIONS

**1. Introduction and Discussion**

Give each student a copy of the student page for Lesson ⊔-10 which includes diagrams to accompany some of the problems. Then tell the children to look at the sample problem and related diagram where they can see three groups of straight lines and ask:

*9*    1   How many straight lines are there altogether?

*3*    2   How many groups of straight lines are there?

*3*    3   How many straight lines are there in each group?

**2. Sample Problem**

Read the following sample problem slowly with the children:

Cheryl bought 9 pencils marked "3 for 20¢."

How much money did she spend altogether?

**3. Major Problem-Solving Approach**

Discuss the problems with the children by asking them the following questions:

*The cost of pencils.*

1   What is the problem about?

*How much money did Cheryl spend for 9 pencils?*

2   What is the question? What do you want to find out to solve the problem?

*Cheryl bought 9 pencils, and 3 pencils cost 20¢.*

3   What do you need to know to solve the problem?

*I will find out how many groups of 3 there are in 9 and multiply my answer by the cost of 3 pencils.*

4  Tell in your own words what you need to do to solve the problem.

*Each straight line in the diagram represents a pencil. There are 9 straight lines altogether, representing the 9 pencils Cheryl bought. These 9 straight lines are divided into 3 groups of 3. The first group of 3 pencils costs 20¢, the second group of 3 pencils costs 20¢, and the third group of 3 pencils costs 20¢. If I add 20¢ three times or multiply 20¢ by three, I will find the total cost for 9 pencils.*

5  How could you use your diagram to find your answer?

$$20¢ + 20¢ + 20¢ = $$
_____ or
$$3 \times 20¢ = $$ _____

6  Write a number sentence for this problem.

7  What do you think your answer will be? Will it be greater or less than 20¢?

8  Find your answer using the diagram.

9  What did you think your answer would be? Is it the same?

*60¢*

10  How much money did Cheryl spend altogether?

Give your answer in a sentence.

*Cheryl spent 60¢ for the 9 pencils.*

Continue this procedure with the student problems for Lesson ⊔-10 that have accompanying diagrams. You may also want to complete a problem together where the students must create their own diagrams. Then let the children do the last few problems on their own. Encourage the children to use the diagrams to help them solve the problems.

**ANSWERS**
**(For Student Problems)**

1  Beth's father will have 4 pieces of wood.

2  They ran 15 laps in all.

3  Yes, Amy will have 4 cupcakes left over.

4  The cake was cut into 16 slices.

5  Jim's father will need to buy 24 yards of fencing.

*Bonus*  Joe ran 270 feet.

Name_____

**SAMPLE PROBLEM**

Cheryl bought 9 pencils marked "3 for 20¢." How much money did she spend altogether?

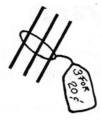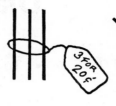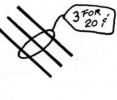

---

1  Beth's father has a piece of wood 8 feet long. He wants to cut it into pieces each 2 feet long. How many pieces will he have when he cuts the wood?

2  Jim, Dave, Randy, Lee, and Tom each ran 3 laps. How many laps did they run in all?

---

3  Amy made 36 cupcakes for the cake sale. She has 4 boxes, and each box holds 8 cupcakes. Will she have any cupcakes left over? If so, how many? (Draw 4 boxes and 8 cupcakes in each.)

4  It is John's birthday today and his mother made him a cake for his party. There were 4 children at the party, and they each ate 4 slices of birthday cake. After the party, there was no more cake left. How many slices was the cake cut into?

---

5  Jim's father is going to the store to buy fencing for their backyard. Their backyard is 8 yards long and 4 yards wide. How many yards of fencing will Jim's father need to buy?

*Bonus*  Joe's Little League team was practicing base running. Joe ran all around the bases two times and then ran to first base before he stopped. If it is 30 feet from base to base, how far did Joe run? (Clue: draw a diagram)

---

**211**

# Lesson □-11 Solving Problems by Drawing Diagrams

PURPOSES
- To draw diagrams to represent problems.

- To use diagrams to solve the word problems.

- To state how the diagrams helped to solve the problems.

- To follow the steps of the major problem-solving approach.

DIRECTIONS

**1. Sample Problem**

Read the following sample problem slowly with the children:

It takes Mr. Logan 1 minute to saw through a log.

How long will it take him to cut the log into 10 pieces?

**2. Major Problem-Solving Approach**

Discuss the problem with the children by asking them the following questions:

*The time it takes to cut a log.*

1  What is the problem about?

*How long will it take Mr. Logan to cut the log into 10 pieces?*

2  What is the question? What do you want to find out to solve the problem?

*It takes Mr. Logan 1 minute to saw through the log, and he wants to cut the log in 10 pieces.*

3  What do you need to know to solve the problem?

*10 pieces.*

4  Instead of drawing a picture about the problem, this time we will draw a diagram. Draw a long line to represent the log Mr. Logan is cutting. (Draw a line on the blackboard.) How many pieces does Mr. Logan want to cut the log into?

(Divide your line into 10 segments or parts.)

*I will count the number of cuts it takes to divide the log into 10 pieces and multiply my answer by 1 to find out how many minutes it takes Mr. Logan.*

5   Tell in your own words what you need to do to solve the problem.

*You can count the number of divisions or cuts you made in your line when you divided it into 10 parts and multiply your answer by 1 to find out how many minutes it took Mr. Logan to cut the log into 10 pieces.*

6   How will I use my diagram to solve the problem?

*Number of cuts*
*× 1 = _____*

7   What do you think your answer will be?

8   Write a number sentence for this problem.

9   Count the number of divisions or cuts in the line. Multiply your answer by 1.

*9 minutes.*

10   What is your answer?

What did you guess your answer would be? Is it the same?

*It will take Mr. Logan 9 minutes to cut the log into 10 pieces.*

11   Give your answer in a sentence.

Follow a similar procedure for the student problems on the next page. You may want to do one or two more together to give the children practice at drawing a diagram of the problem situation. Encourage the children to use the diagrams they have drawn to help solve the problems.

ANSWERS
(For Student Problems)

1   Joe has 20 trees growing in his yard.

2   Philip used 16 eggs to make the cakes.

3   There are 24 books altogether.

4   There are 50 corn plants altogether.

5   Susie could plant 6 plants in the row.

*Bonus*   The girls are 30 meters apart.

Name_____

## SAMPLE PROBLEM

It takes Mr. Logan 1 minute to saw
through a log. How long will it take
him to cut the log into 10 pieces?

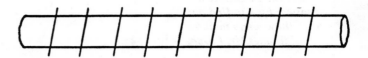

| | |
|---|---|
| 1 Joe has 9 trees growing in his front garden and 11 trees growing in his back garden. How many trees does Joe have altogether? | 2 Philip made 8 cakes for a party. He used 2 eggs in each cake. How many eggs did he use? (Draw a diagram.) |
| 3 There are 6 books in each stack. There are 4 stacks. How many books are there in all? | 4 A field of corn has 5 rows. There are 10 plants in each row. How many corn plants are there? |
| 5 Susie planted some tomato plants. Her row was 16 feet long. She planted one plant at the beginning of the row, and then put the plants 3 feet apart. How many plants could she plant in the row? | *Bonus* 2 girls run in opposite directions, starting from the same point. One girl runs 10 meters, and the other girl runs 20 meters. How far apart are they? |

# Lesson ⊔-12   Solving Problems by Building Tables

**PURPOSES**

- To construct a table for each problem and use the tables to solve the problems.

- To follow the steps of the major problem-solving approach to solve the problems.

**DIRECTIONS**

**1. Sample Problem**

Read the following sample problem slowly with the children:

> Jenny picked between 5 and 8 flowers.
>
> Rita picked twice as many flowers as Jenny picked.
>
> How many flowers could Rita have picked?

**2. Major Problem-Solving Approach**

Discuss the problem with the children by asking them the following questions:

*Picking flowers.*

1  What is the problem about?

*How many flowers could Rita have picked?*

2  What is the question? What do you want to find out to solve the problem?

*Jenny picked between 5 and 8 flowers, and Rita picked twice as many flowers as Jenny picked.*

3  What do you need to know to solve the problem?

*I will multiply the number of flowers Jenny picked by 2; or I will double—add twice—the number of flowers Jenny could have picked to see how many Rita picked.*

4  Tell in your own words how you will solve the problem.

*Because Rita picked twice as many flowers as Jenny picked.*

Why?

*No, Jenny picked between 5 and 8 flowers.*

5  Do you know exactly the number of flowers Jenny picked?

*Rita picked twice as many flowers as Jenny picked and 2 × 5 = 10; or 5 + 5 = 10.*

6  If Jenny picked 5 flowers, how many flowers did Rita pick?

*Rita picked 12 flowers
because 2 × 6 = 12;
or 6 + 6 = 12.*

*Rita picked 14 flowers,
because 2 × 7 = 14;
or 7 + 7 = 14.*

*Rita picked 16 flowers,
because 2 × 8 = 16;
or 8 + 8 = 16.*

7   If Jenny picked 6 flowers, how many flowers did Rita pick?

8   If Jenny picked 7 flowers, how many flowers did Rita pick?

9   If Jenny picked 8 flowers, how many flowers did Rita pick?

10   We can write our answer to this problem in the form of a table. Write this table on the blackboard for the children.

| *Number of flowers Jenny picked* | *Number of flowers Rita picked* |
| --- | --- |
| 5 | 10 |
| 6 | 12 |
| 7 | 14 |
| 8 | 16 |

11   We can state our answer sentences as follows:

If Jenny picked 5 flowers, Rita picked 10 flowers.

If Jenny picked 6 flowers, Rita picked 12 flowers.

If Jenny picked 7 flowers, Rita picked 14 flowers.

If Jenny picked 8 flowers, Rita picked 16 flowers.

Rita picked either 10, 12, 14, or 16 flowers.

Follow a similar procedure with the student problems at the end of the lesson. Construct a table for each problem. You may wish to do some of the problems with the children. The length of the table may be stipulated in the problem; otherwise, the table should be as long as is reasonable. For example, in Problem 5 it is unlikely that a boy would have more than 10 baseballs.

**ANSWERS
(For Students Problems)**

(Verbally state each of the answers as a complete sentence)

*Number of Children*

1

| *Mrs. Scott* | *Mrs. Smith* |
| --- | --- |
| 0 | 2 |
| 1 | 3 |
| 2 | 4 |
| 3 | 5 |
| 4 | 6 |
| 5 | 7 |
| 6 | 8 |

Mrs. Smith has between 2 and 8 children.

*Marble Games Won*

2  Andy                    Sally
   4 ————————————— 1
   5 ————————————— 2
   6 ————————————— 3
   7 ————————————— 4

Sally won between 1 and 4 games.

*Weight in Kilograms*

3  Paul                    Susan
   35 ———————————— 30
   36 ———————————— 31
   37 ———————————— 32
   38 ———————————— 33
   39 ———————————— 34
   40 ———————————— 35

Susan weighs between 30 and 35 kilograms.

*Problems Correct*

4  Janet                   Cindy
   15 ———————————— 17
   16 ———————————— 18
   17 ———————————— 19
   18 ———————————— 20

Cindy got between 17 and 20 problems right on the test.

*Number of Baseballs*

5  John                    Ray
   0 ————————————— 4
   1 ————————————— 5
   2 ————————————— 6
   3 ————————————— 7
   4 ————————————— 8
   5 ————————————— 9

John could have any reasonable number of baseballs, so long as Ray has 4 more.

*Crayons for Each Boy*

**Bonus**  Dave        Steve        Roy
   2 ————— 6 ————— 8
   3 ————— 9 ————— 11
   4 ————— 12 ————— 14
   5 ————— 15 ————— 17

Roy has either 8, 11, 14, or 17 crayons.

Name_____

**SAMPLE PROBLEM**

Jenny picked between 5 and 8

flowers. Rita picked twice as many

flowers as Jenny picked. How many

flowers could Rita have picked?

| | |
|---|---|
| 1  Mrs. Smith has 2 more children than Mrs. Scott has. Mrs. Scott has no more than 6 children. How many children could Mrs. Smith have? (Clue: Make a chart.) | 2  Andy won between 4 and 7 games of marbles. Sally won 3 fewer games than Andy won. How many games could Sally have won? |
| 3  Paul weighs between 35 and 40 kilograms. Susan weighs 5 kilograms less than Paul. How many kilograms could Susan weigh? | 4  Janet got between 15 and 18 problems right on her math tests in January. Cindy got 2 more problems right on each test than did Janet. How many problems did Cindy get right on the tests? |
| 5  Ray has 4 more baseballs than John has. How many baseballs could John have? | *Bonus*  Dave has between 2 and 5 crayons. Steve has 3 times as many crayons as Dave has. Roy has 2 more crayons than Steve has. How many crayons could Roy have? |

# Lesson ⊔-13  Solving Problems from a Graph

PURPOSES
- To solve the problems with the use of a graph.

- To develop the children's ability to discriminate.

- To review the major problem-solving approach.

DIRECTIONS

1. Introduction

Tell the children to look at the graph. (See the Graph for Lesson ⊔-13 at the end of the lesson.) Discuss the graph with them. Tell them that each block represents a box of candy that was sold by one of the girls. The numbers on the left-hand side tell you how many boxes of candy were sold, or you can count the number of blocks above each girl's name.

2. Discussion

Ask the children questions about the graph to give them practice at reading information from it.

1  How many girls sold boxes of candy altogether?

2  What are their names?

3  Who sold the most boxes of candy?

4  Who sold the least boxes of candy?

5  How many boxes of candy did Sally sell?

6  How many boxes of candy did Jane sell?

3. Sample Problem

Read the following sample problem slowly with the children:

How many boxes of candy did Ruth and Carol sell altogether?

4. Major Problem-Solving Approach

*Selling boxes of candy.*

*How many boxes of candy did Ruth and Carol sell altogether?*

Now ask the following questions:

1  What is the problem about?

2  What is the question? What do you want to find out to solve the problem?

| | |
|---|---|
| *The number of boxes Ruth sold and the number of boxes Carol sold.* | 3 What do you need to know to solve the problem? |
| *I will add the number of boxes Ruth sold to the number of boxes Carol sold.* | 4 Tell in your own words how you will solve the problem. |
| *By looking at the graph and counting the number of blocks above Ruth's name.* | 5 How will you find out the number of boxes Ruth sold? |
| *4* | How many blocks did you count? |
| *By looking at the graph and counting the number of blocks above Carol's name.* | 6 How will you find out the number of boxes Carol sold? |
| *11* | How many blocks did you count? |
| *4 + 11 = _____* | 7 Write a number sentence for this problem. |
| | 8 What do you think your answer will be? |
| *I can count the number of blocks above Ruth's name together with the number of blocks above Carol's name.* | 9 How can you use your graph to find the answer? |
| | 10 What did you guess your answer would be? Is it the same? |
| *Ruth and Carol sold 15 boxes of candy altogether.* | 11 Give your answer in a sentence. |

Follow a similar procedure for the student problems on the next page. You may want to do one or two more problems together to give the children practice at reading and using information from a graph. Encourage the children to use the graph to find their answers.

**ANSWERS**
**(For Student Problems)**

1 Fran and Sally sold 20 boxes of candy altogether.

2 Carol sold 9 more boxes of candy than Amy.

3 Fran, Sally, and Carol sold 31 boxes of candy.

4 Tina sold 15 boxes of candy.

5 Sally sold the most boxes (12). This is 10 more boxes than Amy, who sold 2 boxes.

*Bonus* The Girl Scout Troop sold 84 boxes of candy.

**LESSON ⊔-13**                          Name_____

**SAMPLE PROBLEM (The Graph for Lesson ⊔-13 is on the following page.)**

How many boxes of candy did Ruth

and Carol sell altogether?

| | |
|---|---|
| 1  How many boxes of candy did Fran and Sally sell altogether? | 2  How many more boxes did Carol sell than Amy? |
| 3  How many boxes did Fran, Sally, and Carol sell? | 4  Tina sold three times as many boxes as Jane did. How many boxes did Tina sell? |
| 5  How many more boxes did the girl who sold the most amount of candy sell than the girl who sold the least amount of candy? | *Bonus*  The Girl Scout Troop as a whole sold twice as many boxes of candy as the girls shown on the graph. How many boxes of candy did the Girl Scout Troop sell? |

Name_____

# Boxes of Candy Sold

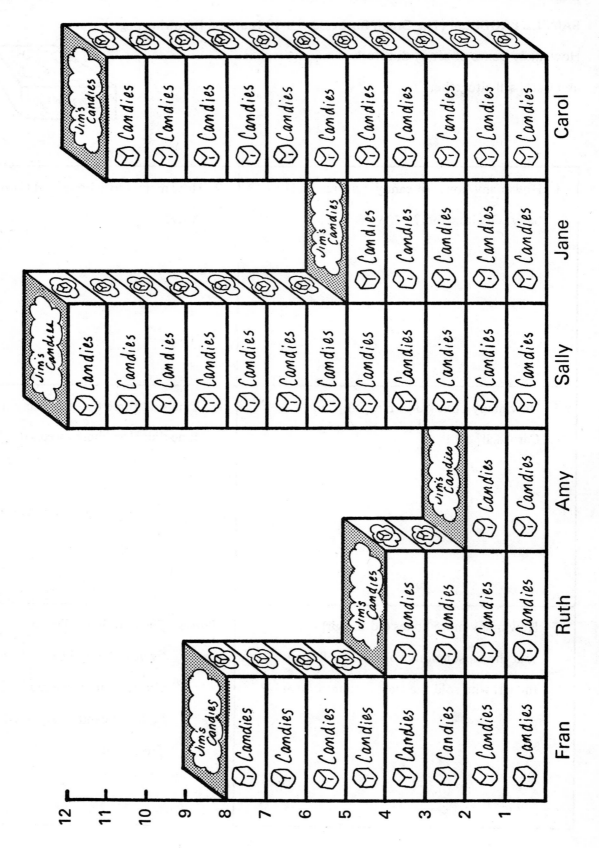

# Lesson ☐-14  Writing and Solving Our Own Problems

PURPOSES

- The children will write their own problems, basing their problems on the following types of number sentences: $a + b = $ _____ ; $a - b = $ _____ ; $a \div b = $ _____ ; $a \times b = $ _____ .

- The children will write their own problems, basing their problems on two numbers only; they can decide for themselves the operation(s) they will use.

- The children will follow the steps of the major problem-solving approach to set up and solve their problems.

## DIRECTIONS

**1. Introduction and Discussion**

Write the following number sentence on the blackboard.

$$2 \times 8 = \text{_____} \quad (\text{or } 8 + 8 = \text{_____})$$

1 Look at the number sentence on the board. Using these numbers, what types of things could we write a problem about? Elicit responses from the children and write some of them down on the blackboard (e.g., marbles, candy, books, pencils).

*2 and 8*

2 What will be the important facts in our problem? What numbers will you use?

*Because they are the numbers given in the number sentence.*

Why?

*I had 8 marbles and John had twice as many; Sue bought 2 candy bars at 8¢ each; I read 2 books a week for 8 weeks; Amy has 2 pencil cases with 8 pencils in each case.*

Put these numbers into sentences to give the important facts in the problem.

*How many marbles does John have? How much money did Sue spend? How many books did I read in 8 weeks? How many pencils does Amy have altogether?*

3 What will our question be?

**2. Sample Problem**    Write one of the problems the children made up on the blackboard:

> I have 8 marbles.
>
> John has twice as many.
>
> How many marbles does John have?

**3. Major Problem-Solving Approach**    Solve this problem following the steps of the major problem-solving approach. (The steps for this procedure are outlined in detail in Chapter 1.)

Continue this procedure for the four number sentences given on the student problem page. Get the children to write down the problem they have made up from the number sentence before solving the problem. For the fifth problem, tell them they can use any operation they like, but they must use the numbers 6 and 7.

**ANSWERS (For Student Problems)**    The answers will vary, depending on the problems devised by each student. Have the children check each other's work to see that problems make sense and answers are correct.

**SAMPLE PROBLEM**

$2 \times 8 =$ _____ (or $8 + 8 =$ _____)

I have 8 marbles. John has twice as
many. How many marbles does John
have?

| | |
|---|---|
| 1  $20 - 9 =$ _____ | 2  $25 + 5 =$ _____ |
| 3  $5 \times 2 =$ _____ | 4  $16 \div 8 =$ _____ |
| 5  Write a problem using the numbers 6 and 7. | *Bonus*  Write a problem using the numbers 2, 3, 4, 500, 600, and 700. |

# Lesson ⊔-15   Using Mathematical Vocabulary

PURPOSES
- To instruct the children in how to solve problems using the following mathematical vocabulary: *half, twice, double, equals, most, least.*

- To review the major problem-solving approach.

DIRECTIONS

**1. Sample Problem**

Read the following sample problem slowly to the children:

> Carol has saved $6 so far to buy a new tennis racket.
>
> This is *half* of the money she needs.
>
> How much money does Carol need?

**2. Major Problem-Solving Approach**

Discuss the problem with the children by asking them the following questions:

*Buying a tennis racket.*

1  What is the problem about?

*How much money does Carol need?*

2  What is the question? What do you want to find out to solve the problem?

*Carol has saved $6, and that is half of the money she needs.*

3  What do you need to know to solve the problem?

*Half.*

*Because "half" means there are two equal parts.*

4  Which word in the problem tells you how to solve it?
Why?

*I will multiply the amount of money Carol has by 2; or I will add $6 and $6 because each is half as much as Carol needs.*

5  Tell in your own words how you would solve this problem?

*2 × $6 = _____*
*or $6 + $6 = _____*

6  Write a number sentence for this problem.

7  Will your answer be greater or less than 12? What do you think your answer will be?

8  Compute your answer.

9 What did you guess your answer would be? Is it the same?

*Carol needs $12 to buy a tennis racket.*

10 Give your answer in a sentence.

Follow a similar procedure with the other problems for Lesson ⊔-15. You may want to do one or two more problems together and then just read the problems to the children, explaining the mathematical terms in them. Discuss all problems orally when the children have finished.

**ANSWERS**
**(For Student Problems)**

1 Sam needs 13 more hats.

2 Fran has saved $26.

3 Gordon delivered the most papers.

4 Lee and Alex worked 21 hours altogether.

5 Mike earned the least money.

*Bonus* He should pay Bill $16 and Sue $8.

Name_____

**SAMPLE PROBLEM**

Carol has saved $6 so far to buy a new

tennis racket. This is *half* of the

money she needs. How much money

does Carol need?

| | |
|---|---|
| 1  It is Sam's birthday today, and he is having a party. 25 children will be coming to the party. Sam is making party hats for them. He has already made 12 party hats. How many more hats does he have to make so that the number of party hats equals the number of children coming to the party? | 2  Joan and Fran are saving to go on vacation. Joan has saved $13, and Fran has saved double the amount of money Joan has saved. How much money has Fran saved? |
| 3  Tina and Gordon both work on a paper route. Last Monday, Tina delivered 8 papers in the morning and 7 papers in the afternoon. On the same day, Gordon delivered 9 papers in the morning and 8 papers in the afternoon. Who delivered the most papers that day? | 4  Lee worked 7 hours last week. Alex worked twice the amount of hours that Lee worked. How many hours did they work altogether? |
| 5  Mike worked 7 hours for $2 an hour. Jim worked 6 hours for $3 an hour. Leslie worked 4 hours for $4 an hour. Who earned the least money? | *Bonus*  Jerry worked on a farm for two days and earned $32. He owed his brother Bill half of what he earned. He also owed his sister Sue half as much as he owed Bill. How much should he pay Bill? How much should he pay Sue? |

# Lesson ⊔-16  Finding Key Words

PURPOSES

- To be able to find the following key words in the problems and relate these words to the appropriate operation(s) in order to solve the problems:

  | | | |
  |---|---|---|
  | "left" | — | subtraction |
  | "altogether" | — | addition or multiplication |
  | "in all" | — | addition or multiplication |

- To review the major problem-solving approach.

DIRECTIONS

**1. Sample Problem**

Read the following sample problem slowly with the children:

> Mary bought 4 boxes of crayons.
>
> There are 12 crayons in each box.
>
> How many crayons did Mary buy *in all*?

**2. Major Problem-Solving Approach**

Discuss the problem with the children by asking them the following questions:

*Crayons.*

1  What is the problem about?

*How many crayons did Mary buy in all?*

2  What is the question?

*Mary bought 4 boxes of crayons, and there are 12 crayons in each box.*

3  What do you need to know to solve the problem?

*I will add the number of crayons in a box together 4 times; or I will multiply the number of crayons in a box by the number of boxes Mary bought.*

4  Tell in your own words what you need to do to solve the problem.

*In all.*

Why will you add (or multiply)? Is there any word or phrase in the problem that lets you know you must add (or multiply) to find your answer?

*Because "in all" usually means putting things together.*

Why?

*12 + 12 + 12 + 12*
*= _____*
*or 4 × 12 = _____*

5  Write a number sentence for this problem.

6  What do you think your answer will be?

7  Compute your answer using your number sentence.

8  What did you think your answer would be? Is it the same?

*Mary bought 48 crayons in all.*

9  Give your answer in a sentence.

Complete the student problems for Lesson ⌴-16 in a similar fashion. Encourage the children to pick out the key word in each of the problems and to relate the appropriate operation(s) to the word.

**ANSWERS**
**(For Student Problems)**

1  Tom has 12 nails left.

2  Tom put 27 books on the shelves.

3  Tom put up 15 shelves in all.

4  Tom has $2.50 left.

5  Tom spent 10 hours putting up the shelves.

*Bonus*  The boards for Tom's shelves cost $66 in all.

**LESSON ⊔-16**

**SAMPLE PROBLEM**

Mary bought 4 boxes of crayons.

There are 12 crayons in each box.

How many crayons did Mary buy

*in all*?

---

**1**  Tom is putting up shelves. He had 26 nails and he used 14 of them. How many nails does Tom have left?

**2**  Tom put 12 books on the first shelf, 8 books on the second shelf, and 7 books on the third shelf. How many books did he put on the shelves altogether?

---

**3**  There are 8 rooms in Tom's house. Tom put 3 shelves in 5 of the rooms. How many shelves did Tom put up in all?

**4**  Tom had $10. He bought a hammer for $5.50 and some nails for $2. How much money does Tom have left?

---

**5**  It takes Tom 2 hours to put up 3 shelves. He put up 9 shelves on Monday and 6 shelves on Tuesday. How many hours did he spend putting up shelves altogether?

***Bonus***  The boards for Tom's shelves cost $1.10 per foot. Each of the 15 shelves was 4 feet long. How much did the boards cost in all?

---

231

# Lesson ⊔-17   Finding Key Phrases

PURPOSES

- To provide instruction in determining the following key phrases in the problems and to relate these phrases to the appropriate operations in order to solve the problems:

| | |
|---|---|
| "how many more" | — subtraction |
| "difference between" | — subtraction |
| "together they have" | — addition |
| "... times" | — addition or multiplication |

- To review the major problem-solving approach.

DIRECTIONS

**1. Sample Problem**    Read the following sample problem slowly with the children:

> Joan earned $5.50 babysitting.
>
> Anne earned $4.50 for mowing lawns.
>
> *Together they have* how much money?

**2. Major Problem-Solving Approach**    Discuss the problem with the children by asking them the following questions:

*Earning money.*    1  What is the problem about?

*How much money do Joan and Anne have?*    2  What is the question?

*Joan earned $5.50, and Anne earned $4.50.*    3  What do you need to know to solve the problem?

*I will add the amount of money Joan earned to the amount of money Anne earned.*    4  Tell in your own words what you need to do to solve the problem.

*Together they have.*    Why will you add? Is there any word or phrase in the problem that lets you know you must add to find your answer?

*Because "together" means joining.*    Why?

*$5.50 + $4.50 = _____*    5  Write a number sentence for this problem.

6  What do you think your answer will be?

7 Compute your answer using your number sentence.

8 What did you think your answer would be? Is it the same?

*Joan and Anne together have $10.*

9 Give your answer in a sentence.

Complete the problems for Lesson ⊔-17 in a similar fashion. Encourage the children to pick out the key phrase in each problem and to relate the appropriate operation(s) to the phrase.

**ANSWERS**
**(For Student Problems)**

1 The boys live 15 miles from school.

2 Each day 9 more boys than girls travel to school by bus.

3 There is 1 more girl on the bus.

4 It takes 27 minutes less to get to school from Robin's house.

5 There are 25 children on the bus.

*Bonus* Altogether 27 children had muddy clothes.

**LESSON ⊔-17**

Name_____

**SAMPLE PROBLEM**

Joan earned $5.50 babysitting. Anna earned $4.50 for mowing lawns. *Together they have* how much money?

| | |
|---|---|
| 1  Robin, Sally, Joe, and Gordon travel to school by bus every day. The girls live 5 miles from the school, and the boys live 3 times as far. How far from the school do the boys live? | 2  Every day the bus carries 19 girls and 28 boys to school. What is the difference between the number of boys that travel by bus to school and the number of girls? |
| 3  There are 6 boys and 8 girls on the bus. The bus stops to pick up 4 more boys and 3 more girls. How many more girls than boys are on the bus now? | 4  It takes the bus 40 minutes to go from Joe's house to the school. It takes the bus only 13 minutes to go from Robin's house to the school. What is the difference between the time it takes the bus to go from Joe's house to the school and the time it takes to go from Robin's house to the school? |
| 5  There are 5 girls on the bus. There are 4 times as many boys on the bus as there are girls. How many children are on the bus altogether? | *Bonus*  One day the school bus got stuck, and the driver said the students would have to get out and push. In all, there were 24 boys and 18 girls pushing. Before the bus got loose, half of the girls and two times that many boys got mud all over their clothes. Altogether the bus brought how many children to school with muddy clothes? |

234

# Lesson ⊔-18   Problem Solving and Vocabulary Instruction

**PURPOSES**

- To introduce the children to problems containing two or more different sets, all of which belong to a larger universal set, including:

| | | |
|---|---|---|
| spiders and ladybugs | — | insects |
| onions, potatoes, carrots | — | vegetables |
| oranges, bananas, peaches, apples | — | fruit |
| 1 dozen | — | 12 items |
| a week | — | 7 days |
| a year | — | 12 months |

- To review the major problem-solving approach.

**DIRECTIONS**

**1. Sample Problem**

Read the following sample problem slowly with the children:

Amy went to the store and bought 2 dozen eggs.

How many eggs did she buy altogether?

**2. Major Problem-Solving Approach**

Discuss the problem with the children by asking them the following questions:

*Buying eggs.*

1   What is the problem about?

*How many eggs did Amy buy altogether?*

2   What is the question?

*Amy bought 2 dozen eggs.*

3   What do you need to know to solve the problem?

*12*

4   How many eggs are there in one dozen?

*I will add the number of eggs in one dozen together twice; or I will multiply the number of eggs in one dozen by 2.*

5   Tell in your own words how you will solve this problem.

*$12 + 12 = $_____
or $2 \times 12 = $_____*

6   Write a number sentence for this problem.

7   What do you think your answer will be?

8  Compute your answer.

9  What did you think your answer would be? Is it the same?

*Amy bought 24 eggs altogether.*

10  Give your answer in a sentence.

**ANSWERS**
**(For Student Problems)**

1  Andy and Dave collected 23 insects.

2  Susan writes 28 letters each week.

3  Rick bought 22 vegetables.

4  Jordan reads 72 books in a year.

5  Sadie and Anna used 33 pieces of fruit in the salad.

*Bonus*  46 pieces of fruit and vegetables were bought in all.

Name_____

**SAMPLE PROBLEM**

Amy went to the store and bought

2 dozen eggs. How many eggs did

she buy altogether?

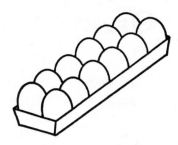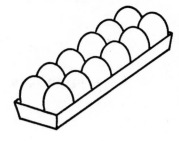

| | |
|---|---|
| 1   Andy and Dave went on a nature walk. They collected 9 spiders and 14 ladybugs. How many insects did they collect altogether? | 2   Susan writes 4 letters every day. How many letters does she write in a week? |
| 3   Rick went to the store to buy some vegetables. He bought 7 potatoes, 10 carrots, and 5 onions. How many vegetables did Rick buy in all? | 4   Jordan reads 6 books a month. How many books does he read in a year? |
| 5   Sadie and Anna are having a party. They are making a fruit salad. They used 6 oranges, 8 bananas, 12 apples, and 7 peaches. The fruit cost them $6 altogether. How many pieces of fruit did they use in the salad? | *Bonus*   Last week Sara's mother made food for three picnics. She bought 14 potatoes, 6 carrots, 1 large onion, 10 bananas, 6 peaches, 5 apples, and 4 oranges. They cost $17.43. How many fruit and vegetable pieces were bought in all? |

# Lesson ☐-19 Money Problems Presented Orally

**PURPOSES**

- To develop the children's listening skills by reading to them simple oral problems, which they will solve mentally.

- To review the major problem-solving approach when presenting oral money problems to the children.

**DIRECTIONS**

**1. Introduction and Discussion**

Discuss money with the children using coins such as pennies, nickels, dimes, and quarters. Make sure that the children know how many cents (pennies) are in a dollar, how many quarters are in a dollar, etc.

**2. Sample Problem**

Tell the children that you are going to read a sample problem to them and you want them to tell you what the problem is about.

Joe had 25¢.

He spent 15¢ in the store.

How much money does Joe have left?

**3. Major Problem-Solving Approach**

Read the problem once and ask the children:

*Money or cents.*

1 What is the problem about?

*How much money does Joe have left?*

2 What is the question?

**4. Continue the Major Problem-Solving Approach**

Reread the problem once again and ask the children:

*Joe had 25¢ and he spent 15¢.*

3 What do you need to know to solve the problem?

*Take the number of cents Joe spent away from the number of cents he had in the beginning.*

4 Tell in your own words what you need to do to solve the problem.

$25¢ - 15¢ = $ _____

5 Do this subtraction in your head without writing anything down on your paper.

*Joe has 10¢ left.*

6 Write only the answer on your paper.

Tell the children that you are going to read five or six more problems to them. (The students do not need to receive copies of the student page for Lesson ⊔-19; however, this is at the option of the classroom teacher.) At the first reading, they should listen to find out what the problem is about and what the question is. The second time, they should listen carefully for the important facts they need to know to solve the problem. Then ask the children to decide how to solve the problem and think out the answer in their heads. Have them write the answer on their papers.

**ANSWERS**
**(For Student Problems)**

1 John has 40¢.

2 Patty has 90¢.

3 Doug has 5¢ left.

4 Sharon needed 40¢ more.

5 Bob has 25¢ left.

*Bonus* Jackie has 50¢ left.

Name_____

**SAMPLE PROBLEM**

Joe had 25¢. He spent 15¢ in the

store. How much money does Joe

have left?

| | |
|---|---|
| 1  John has 8 nickels. How many cents does John have altogether? | 2  Pattie has 9 dimes. How many cents does Pattie have altogether? |
| 3  Doug had a quarter and a dime. He bought an ice cream cone for 30¢. How much money does he have left? | 4  Sharon has 2 quarters. She is saving to buy a ring for 90¢. How much more money does she need? |
| 5  Bob had 3 quarters and 2 dimes. He bought a toy car for 70¢. How much money does Bob have left? | *Bonus*  Jackie had 2 quarters, 3 dimes, 3 nickels, and 5 pennies. She spent 50¢ for a toy airplane. How much money does Jackie have left? |

# Lesson ⊔-20  Shopping Problems Presented Orally

PURPOSES

PURPOSES

- To review the major problem-solving approach by presenting oral problems to the children based on the theme "shopping."

- To develop the children's listening skills by reading to them simple oral problems, which they will solve mentally.

- To develop the children's ability to discriminate by requiring that they find out the prices of the articles from a price list.

## DIRECTIONS

### 1. Introduction and Discussion

Show the children the price list (Price List for Lesson ⊔-20 at the end of the lesson) and discuss it with them. What can you buy? How much does _____ cost?

### 2. Sample Problem

Read the following sample problem to the children twice; after each reading, ask the questions indicated below:

> Jim bought 4 pairs of socks and a pair of gloves.
>
> How much money did Jim spend?

### 3. Major Problem-Solving Approach

After the first reading, ask the children the following questions:

*Buying socks and gloves.*

1  What is the problem about?

*How much money did Jim spend?*

2  What is the question?

### 4. Continue the Major Problem-Solving Approach

Reread the problem once again and ask the children:

*The price of a pair of socks, the price of a pair of gloves; Jim bought 4 pairs of socks and 1 pair of gloves.*

3  What do you need to know to solve the problem?

*By looking at the price list.*

**4** How will you find out the price of a pair of socks and a pair of gloves?

*I will multiply the price of a pair of socks by the number of pairs Jim bought and add my answer to the price of 1 pair of gloves.*

**5** Tell in your own words how you will solve this problem.

*$2*

**6** How much is a pair of socks?

*$3*

How much is a pair of gloves?

*Jim spent $11.*

**7** Do this multiplication and addition in your head and write only the answers on your paper.

Tell the children that you are going to read five or six more problems to them. (The students do not need to receive copies of the student page for Lesson ⊔-20; however, this is at the option of the classroom teacher.) The first time, they should listen to find out what the problem is about and listen carefully for the question. On the second reading, they must listen for the important facts they need to know to solve the problem and use the price list to find out the prices of the articles in the problems.

**ANSWERS**
**(For Student Problems)**

**1** Sue has $4 left.

**2** I could buy 4 umbrellas for $20.

**3** Sally can buy 5 pairs of socks.

**4** Mary has $3 left.

**5** Allen has $4 left.

***Bonus*** Sara and her dad had $7 left.

**SAMPLE PROBLEM** (see the Price List for Lesson ⊔-20 on the next page)

Jim bought 4 pairs of socks and a pair

of gloves. How much money did Jim

spend?

| | |
|---|---|
| 1   Sue has $20.00. She bought 4 rainhats. How much money does Sue have left? | 2   How many umbrellas could you buy for $20? |
| 3   Sally has $11. How many pairs of socks can she buy? | 4   Mary had $30. She bought a pair of boots and a pair of shoes. How much money does she have left? |
| 5   Allen had $25. He bought 2 pairs of gloves and 3 umbrellas. How much money does Allen have left? | *Bonus*   Sara and her dad went shopping for school clothes. He said the most Sara could spend was $85. She needed 6 pairs of socks, 3 pairs of shoes, 1 pair of boots, an umbrella, a rainhat, and 2 pairs of gloves. Was $85 enough money? How much money did they have left, if any? |

Name_____

# Go Shopping

gloves
$3 a pair

socks
$2 a pair

rainhats
$4 each

umbrellas
$5 each

boots
$15 a pair

shoes
$12 a pair

# Lesson ⊔-21   Using Pictures To Help Solve Problems

**PURPOSES**

- To draw simple pictures or use manipulatives to help solve problems.

- To review the major problem-solving approach.

**DIRECTIONS**

**1. Sample Problem**

Give the children copies of the problems for Lesson ⊔-21. Then read the problem about the gingerbread men with them.

> Al made 15 gingerbread men.
>
> 6 were eaten.
>
> How many are left?

**2. Major Problem-Solving Approach**

Discuss the problem with the children by asking them the following questions:

*Gingerbread men.*

1   What is the problem about?

*How many gingerbread men are left?*

2   What is the question?

*Al made 15 gingerbread men, and 6 were eaten.*

3   What do you need to know to solve the problem?

*I will take the number of gingerbread men that were eaten away from the number of gingerbread men Al made.*

4   Tell in your own words how you will solve this problem.

   If necessary, the teacher could draw a picture of the gingerbread men, or help the children to use manipulatives as they solve the problem.

*15 − 6 = _____*

5   Write a number sentence for this problem.

6   What do you think your answer will be?

7   Compute your answer.

8   Compare your answer with your estimation.

*There are 9 gingerbread men left.*

9   Give your answer in a sentence.

You may wish to do another problem from Lesson ⊔-21 together and then let the children do the last few problems on their own. You may read all the problems with the children before they attempt to solve them on their own.

**ANSWERS**
**(For Student Problems)**

1  There are 12 eggs in all.

2  Gail had 23 insects.

3  Sara had 54 fish.

4  Andy and Ray watch 49 hours of TV each week.

5  Mary still has 25 balloons to blow up.

*Bonus*  The dog eats 7 cans of dog food in 3 weeks.

**SAMPLE PROBLEM**

Al made 15 gingerbread men. 6 were

eaten. How many are left? (Hint:  Draw a picture of 15 gingerbread men.)

| | |
|---|---|
| 1  There are 3 birds. Each bird has 4 eggs in its nest. How many eggs are there in all? (Hint: Draw a picture.) | 2  Gail collected 14 bees and 9 beetles. How many insects did she collect in all? |
| 3  Sara had 6 aquariums. Each aquarium had 9 fish in it. How many fish did she have altogether? | 4  Andy watches television for 4 hours every day. Roy watches television for 3 hours every day. How many hours do they both spend watching television in a week? |
| 5  Mary bought a bag of 50 balloons. She blew up 12 in the morning and 13 in the afternoon. How many balloons does she still have to blow up? | *Bonus*  John's dog eats a can of dog food every 3 days. How many cans of dog food does the dog eat in 3 weeks? |

247

# Lesson □-22  Solving Problems by Drawing Pictures

PURPOSES

- To show students how to draw a picture about each problem and to use their picture to help solve the problem.

- To review the major problem-solving approach.

### DIRECTIONS

**1. Sample Problem**

Read the following sample problem slowly to the children:

> 5 children went picking oranges.
>
> They each picked 8 oranges.
>
> How many oranges did they pick in all?

**2. Major Problem-Solving Approach**

Discuss the problem with the children by asking them the following questions:

*Picking oranges.*

1  What is the problem about?

*How many oranges did the children pick in all?*

2  What is the question?

*5 children went picking oranges, and they each picked 8 oranges.*

3  What do you need to know to solve the problem?

4  Draw a picture about the problem. (Make your drawings simple.)

*5*

5  Describe what you have drawn. How many children did you draw?

*8*

How many oranges have you drawn beside each child?

*I will add the number of oranges each child picked 5 times; or I will multiply the number of oranges each child picked by the number of children.*

6  Tell in your own words what you need to do to solve the problem.

*8 + 8 + 8 + 8 + 8 = _____*

*or 5 × 8 = _____*

7  Write a number sentence for this problem.

*I will count the number of oranges I have drawn altogether.*

8  How will you use your picture to solve the problem?

Why?

*Because I drew 8 oranges beside each child.*

9  What do you think your answer will be?

10  Find your answer using your picture.

11  Is your answer the same as your estimation?

*The children picked 40 oranges in all.*

12  Give your answer in a sentence.

Follow a similar procedure for the problems from Lesson ⊔-22. You may want to do one or two more together to give the children practice at drawing a picture of the problem. Encourage the children to use the pictures they have drawn to help them to solve the problem.

**ANSWERS (For Student Problems)**

1  John and Peter caught 25 fish.

2  Joan has 17 more comic books.

3  2 children will have to read from each book.

4  Father was away from home 7½ hours.

5  Dora has 5 beads left.

*Bonus*  Each child should get 3 crayons, and the teacher will have 5 left.

Name_____

**SAMPLE PROBLEM**

5 children went picking oranges.

They each picked 8 oranges. How

many oranges did they pick in all?

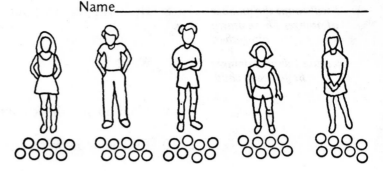

---

1  John and Peter went fishing. John caught

   12 fish, and Peter caught 13 fish. How many

   fish did they catch in all?

2  Joan has 26 comic books, and Mary has 9

   comic books. How many more comic books

   does Joan have?

---

3  The teacher wants to read a story with the

   children. There are 20 children altogether,

   but the teacher has only 10 books for them.

   If the teacher shares the books with the

   children equally, how many children will

   have to read from each book?

4  Father left the house to go to work at

   8:00 a.m. He had lunch at 12:00 and

   arrived home again at 3:30 p.m. How

   many hours was he away from home?

---

5  Dora bought 50 beads to make some

   necklaces and bracelets. She used 25 beads

   to make 1 necklace, and she made 2

   bracelets using 10 beads in each bracelet.

   How many beads does Dora have left?

*Bonus*  The teacher has 80 color crayons to

   give to the 25 children in the class. If

   they are shared equally, how many

   crayons should each student get?

---

# Lesson □-23  Solving Problems from Related Diagrams

PURPOSES

- To show children how to use given diagrams to solve the problems.

- To review the major problem-solving approach.

DIRECTIONS

**1. Introduction and Discussion**

Tell the children to look at the drawing under the sample problem on the student problem page where they can see 2 rectangular crates with circles, to represent oranges, inside of them.

*2*

How many rectangles or crates are there?

*18*

How many circles, which represent oranges, are there in each rectangle?

**2. Sample Problem**

Read the following sample problem to the children:

John's father is packing oranges into crates.

Each crate holds 18 oranges.

How many oranges will 2 crates hold?

**3. Major Problem-Solving Approach**

*Packing oranges into crates.*

*How many oranges will 2 crates hold?*

*Each crate holds 18 oranges.*

*Each rectangle represents a crate, and each circle represents an orange. There are 18 circles in both rectangles; so if I count the total number of circles, I will find my answer.*

Discuss the problem with the children by asking them the following questions:

1  What is the problem about?

2  What is the question?

3  What do you need to know to solve the problem?

4  How could you use the diagram to find your answer?

*Add together the number of oranges one crate holds twice; or multiply the number of oranges one crate holds by 2.*

$18 + 18 = $ _____
or $2 \times 18 = $ _____

*2 crates will hold 36 oranges.*

5  Tell in your own words what you need to do to solve the problem.

6  Write a number sentence for this problem.

7  What do you think your answer will be?

8  Find your answer using the diagram.

9  Compare your answer with your estimation.

10  Give your answer in a sentence.

Continue this procedure with the other problems from Lesson ⊔-23. Do a problem together in which a diagram needs to be drawn, and then let the children do the remaining problems on their own (after the problems have been read aloud to them). If necessary, assist the children as they draw the related diagrams.

ANSWERS
(For Student Problems)

1  The students checked out 20 books.

2  Mary and Sue spent 7 hours at the lake.

3  Max bought 12 crayons.

4  Sally spent 36¢ on candy.

5  Peter traveled 36 miles.

**LESSON ⊔-23**

Name_____

**SAMPLE PROBLEM**

John's father is packing oranges into crates. Each crate holds 18 oranges. How many oranges will 2 crates hold?

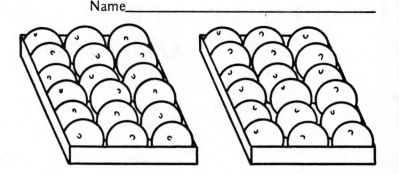

---

1   4 students checked 5 books each out of the library. How many books did the students check out in all?

2   Mary and Sue went to the lake for the day. They arrived there at 11:00 a.m. and left at 6:00 p.m. How many hours did they spend at the lake?

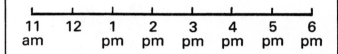

---

3   Max bought some crayons marked "4 for 10¢." He spent 30¢. How many crayons did he buy? (Draw the crayons and mark each group of 4 at 10¢.)

4   Sally bought 6 pieces of candy marked "3 for 10¢" and 6 pieces of candy marked "3 for 8¢." How much money did she spend altogether?

---

5   Peter traveled 16 miles to a restaurant. He then traveled 8 miles to a park and returned home by a shortcut, which was 12 miles. How many miles did Peter travel?

*Bonus*   Make up a problem of your own and draw a diagram of it. Then share it with someone else in your class.

---

# Lesson ☐-24   Solving Problems by Drawing Diagrams

**PURPOSES**
- To help students draw simple diagrams about problems and to use their diagrams to solve the problems.

- To review the major problem-solving approach.

**DIRECTIONS**

**1. Sample Problem**

Read the following problem slowly to the children:

> Linda bought 20 marbles marked "5 for 6¢."
>
> How much money did she spend altogether?

**2. Major Problem-Solving Approach**

Discuss the problem with the children by asking them the following questions:

*Marbles.*

1   What is the problem about?

*How much money did Linda spend altogether?*

2   What is the question?

*Linda bought 20 marbles marked "5 for 6¢."*

3   What do you need to know to solve the problem?

4   This time we will draw a diagram. Let a circle (○) represent a marble.

*5*

How many circles will I draw for 5 marbles?

*6¢*

How much money do these 5 marbles cost?

*4*

How many groups of 5 are there in 20?

I can represent the 20 marbles Linda bought by drawing 4 groups of 5 circles. Each group costs 6¢.

○○○○○ ○○○○○ ○○○○○ ○○○○○
6¢ 6¢ 6¢ 6¢

*Find out how many groups of 5 marbles there are in 20 marbles and multiply my answer by 6¢ because each group of 5 marbles costs 6¢.*

5   Tell in your own words what you need to do to solve the problem.

*From the diagram you can see that there are 4 groups of 5 circles in 20 circles. Each group of 5 circles costs 6¢, so if I add 6¢ together 4 times or multiply 6¢ by 4, I will find the answer.*

$20 \div 5 =$ _____
$\times\ 6\text{¢} =$ _____ ¢

**2**

*Division and multiplication.*

*Linda spent 24¢ altogether.*

6 How will I use my diagram to solve the problem?

7 Write a number sentence for this problem.

8 How many operations (steps) are in this problem? What are they?

9 What do you think your answer will be?

10 Compute your answer.

11 Compare your answer with your estimation.

12 Give your answer in a sentence.

Follow a similar procedure with the other problems for Lesson ⊔-24. You may want to do one more problem together to give the children practice at drawing a diagram of the problem situation. Encourage the children to use the diagrams they have drawn to help them to solve the problem.

**ANSWERS**
**(For Student Problems)**

1 You can make 30 bowls of soup.

2 They will need 6 boxes.

3 Paul spent $3 for the oranges.

4 Nancy traveled for 4 hours.

5 Jim has 36¢ left.

*Bonus* Sally spent $6.21 for apples.

**LESSON ⎵-24**

Name_____

**SAMPLE PROBLEM**

Linda bought 20 marbles marked
"5 for 6¢." How much money did
she spend altogether?

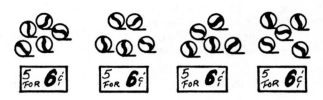

---

1  You can make 5 bowls of soup from one package of soup mix. How many bowls of soup can you make from 6 packages?

2  The Simpsons are moving to a new house. They are packing their books into boxes. Each box holds 8 books. How many boxes will they need for 48 books?

---

3  Paul bought 18 oranges marked "6 for $1." How much money did he spend?

4  Nancy traveled 50 miles at a speed of 25 miles per hour. She then quickened her speed and went 100 miles at a speed of 50 miles per hour. How many hours did Nancy travel?

---

5  Jim had $1. He bought 24 pieces of candy marked "3 for 8¢." How much money does Jim have left?

*Bonus*  Sally bought 27 apples marked "3 for 69¢." How much money did she spend?

# Lesson ⬜-25    Solving Problems by Building Tables

**PURPOSES**

- To instruct children in how to solve problems by building tables.

- To review the major problem-solving approach.

**DIRECTIONS**

**1. Sample Problem**

Read the following sample problem slowly to the children:

> Rita has twice as many brothers as Mary has.
>
> How many brothers could Rita have?

**2. Major Problem-Solving Approach**

Discuss the problem with the children by asking them the following questions:

*Brothers.*

1   What is the problem about?

*How many brothers could Rita have?*

2   What is the question?

*The number of brothers Mary has and that Rita has twice as many brothers as Mary has.*

3   What do you need to know to solve the problem?

*I will multiply the number of brothers Mary has by 2; or I will double the number of brothers Mary has.*

4   Tell in your own words how you will solve the problem.

*Because Rita has twice as many brothers as Mary.*

Why?

*No.*

5   Do you know how many brothers Mary has?

We can find the answer to this problem by using a table. (Write this table on the blackboard for the children.)

| Number of Brothers Mary Has | Number of Brothers Rita Has |
| --- | --- |
| 0 | 0 |
| 1 | 2 |
| 2 | 4 |
| 3 | 6 |
| 4 | 8 |

6 We can state our answer sentences as follows:

If Mary has no brothers, Rita has no brothers.

If Mary has 1 brother, Rita has 2 brothers.

If Mary has 2 brothers, Rita has 4 brothers.

If Mary has 3 brothers, Rita has 6 brothers.

If Mary has 4 brothers, Rita has 8 brothers.

Follow a similar procedure to solve the other problems for Lesson ⌐-25. Construct a table for each problem. You may wish to do one or two more problems together with the children if they have not had much previous experience at constructing tables. The length of the table may be stipulated in the problem, or the table should be as long as is reasonable. For example, in the above problem, it is unlikely that Rita would have more than 8 brothers.

**ANSWERS**
**(For Student Problems)**

1 Lisa is between 4 ft. 3 in. and 4 ft. 9 in. tall.

2 Sandy has 18, 21, 24, 27, or 30 model cars.

3 Jonathan has $1, $2, $3, $4, or $5.

4 The bus might travel between 100 and 150 miles.

5 It takes Jim between 12 and 18 minutes to walk to the store.

*Bonus* Peter could have scored from 10 to 20 points.

Name_____

**SAMPLE PROBLEM**

Rita has twice as many brothers as

Mary has. How many brothers could

Rita have?

| Mary's brothers | Rita's brothers |
|---|---|
| 0 —————— | 0 |
| 1 —————— | 2 |
| 2 —————— | 4 |
| 3 —————— | 6 |
| 4 —————— | 8 |

---

1  Sue is between 4 ft. and 4 ft. 6 in. tall. Lisa is 3 inches taller than Sue. How tall is Lisa? (Build a table to show how tall the girls are.)

2  Ron has between 6 and 10 model cars. Sandy has three times as many model cars as Ron has. How many model cars does Sandy have?

---

3  Jan has four times as much money as Jonathan. Jan has either $4, $8, $12, $16, or $20. How much money could Jonathan have?

4  Susan's family was going for an automobile trip. They were going to travel between 20 and 30 miles. On their way, a bus passed them. It was going five times as far as they were. How far might the bus be traveling?

---

5  It takes Joan between 6 and 9 minutes to walk to the store. It takes Sam 7 more minutes to walk to the store than it takes Joan. It takes Jim twice as long to walk to the store as it takes Joan. How many minutes does it take Jim to walk to the store?

*Bonus*  Amy scored between 10 and 15 on her spelling test. Mary scored 5 points less than Amy. Peter scored twice as many points as Mary. How many points could Peter have scored?

---

# Lesson ⊔-26   Solving Problems from a Graph

- To help students to solve problems by using information from a graph.

- To review the major problem-solving approach.

## DIRECTIONS

### 1. Introduction

Tell the children to look at the weather map (see Weather Graph for Lesson ⊔-26 at the end of the lesson) and discuss it with them. Tell them that each block represents a day in one of the three months September, October, or November. The numbers on the left-hand side tell you how many sunny days, or cloudy days, or rainy days, etc. there were in these months.

### 2. Discussion

Ask the children questions about the graph to give them practice at reading information from it such as:

*Sunny, cloudy, rainy, windy, snowy, and frosty days.*

1   What kinds of days did we have in September, October, and November?

*Sunny days.*

2   What kind of day did we have the most often?

*15*

3   How many windy days did we have?

### 3. Sample Problem

Read the following sample problem to the children:

How many rainy days and windy days were there in September, October, and November?

### 4. Major Problem-Solving Approach

Discuss the problem with the children by asking them the following questions:

*Rainy days and windy days.*

1   What is the problem about?

*How many rainy days and windy days were there in September, October, and November?*

2   What is the question?

*The number of rainy days and the number of windy days in September, October, and November.*

3   What do you need to know to solve the problem?

*I will add the number of rainy days to the number of windy days.*

4  Tell in your own words how you will solve the problem.

*By looking at the graph and counting the number of blocks above where it says "Rainy days."*

5  How will you find out the number of rainy days?

*10*

How many blocks did you count?

How will you find out the number of windy days?

*By looking at the graph and counting the number of blocks above where it says "Windy days."*

*15*

How many blocks did you count?

*10 + 15 = _____*

6  Write a number sentence for this problem.

7  What do you think your answer will be?

*I can count the number of blocks above "Rainy days" and "Windy days."*

8  How can you use your graph to find the answer?

9  What did you guess your answer would be? Is it the same?

*There were 25 rainy days and windy days in September, October, and November.*

10  Give your answer in a sentence.

Follow a similar procedure for the other problems in Lesson ⊔-26. You may want to do one or two more problems together to give the children practice at reading and using information from a graph. Encourage the children to use the graph to find their answers.


ANSWERS
(For Student Problems)

1  There were 14 more sunny days.

2  There were 36 cloudy and frosty days.

3  There were 24 sunny days.

4  We had sunny days the most often and snowy days the least often.

5  There were 31 rainy, snowy, and windy days.

*Bonus*  There were 4 sunny days for each snowy day.

**SAMPLE PROBLEM** (See the Weather Graph for Lesson ⊔-26 on the next page.)

How many rainy days and windy days

were there in September, October,

and November?

| | |
|---|---|
| 1  How many more sunny days were there than rainy days? | 2  How many cloudy days and frosty days were there in all? |
| 3  There were 4 times as many sunny days as snowy days. How many sunny days were there? | 4  Which kind of day did we have the most often? Which kind of day did we have the least often? |
| 5  How many rainy, windy, and snowy days were there altogether? | *Bonus*  How many sunny days were there for each snowy day? |

Name_____

# Weather Graph
## for September, October, and November

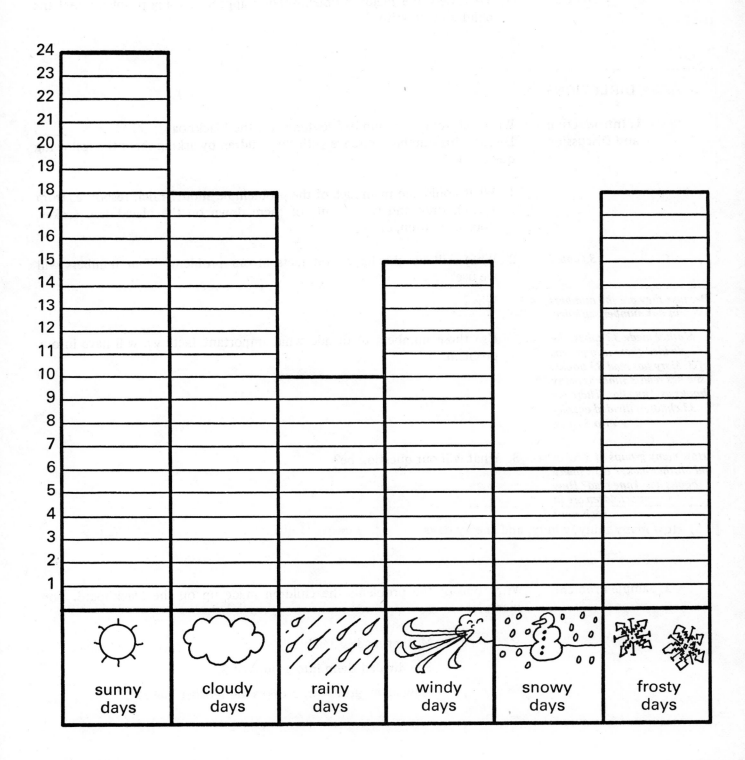

# Lesson ⊔-27 Writing and Solving Our Own Problems

PURPOSE

- To review the major problem-solving approach using problems that the children will write.

DIRECTIONS

**1. Introduction and Discussion**

Write the following number sentence on the blackboard: $33 \div 3 = \underline{\hspace{1cm}}$. Discuss this number sentence with the children by asking them the following questions:

1 What could the main idea of the problem be about? Elicit responses from the children and write some of them down on the blackboard (cakes, books, children, etc.).

*33 and 3*

2 What will be the important facts in our problem? What numbers will we use?

*Because they are the numbers in our number sentence.*

Why?

*Mother made 33 cakes; she divided them into groups of 3. Mary has read 33 books; she has read 3 times as many books as Anne has. There are 33 children divided equally into 3 rows.*

Use these numbers to decide what important facts we will have in our problem.

*How many groups of 3 cakes did Mother make? How many books has Anne read? How many children are in each row?*

3 What will our question be?

**2. Sample Problem**

Write one of the problems the children made up on the blackboard. For example:

> Mother made 33 cakes.
>
> She divided them into groups of 3.
>
> How many groups of 3 cakes did Mother make?

**3. Major Problem-Solving Approach**

Solve this problem following the steps of the major problem-solving approach. (The steps for this procedure are outlined in Chapter 1.)

Follow a similar procedure for the other number sentences on the student page of Lesson ⊔-27. You may wish to complete another problem with the children if they have not had much prior experience in writing their own problems. The students may also make use of pictures, diagrams, and other aids if they find them helpful.

**ANSWERS (For Student Problems)**

The answers will vary depending on the problems devised by each student. Have the children check each other's work to see that problems make sense and answers are correct.

Name_____

**SAMPLE PROBLEM**

$33 \div 3 =$ _____. Mother made 33 cakes.

She divided them into groups of 3. How

many groups of 3 cakes did Mother make?

(Write problems about the following number sentences. If you need help with spelling, ask your teacher.)

| | |
|---|---|
| 1 $15 + 17 =$ _____ | 2 $27 - 19 =$ _____ |
| 3 $7 \times 9 =$ _____ | 4 $36 \div 4 =$ _____ |
| 5 Write a problem using the numbers 3, 8, and 9. | **Bonus**  $(3 + 6) \times 7 =$ _____ |

# Lesson ☐-28  Solving Two-Step Problems and Problems with Unnecessary Information

**PURPOSES**

- To provide practice in solving two-step problems and problems containing unnecessary information.

- To review the major problem-solving approach.

**DIRECTIONS**

**1. Sample Problem**

Read the following sample problem slowly to the children:

> Eddie made 2 batches of cakes.
>
> There were 10 cakes in the first batch and 9 cakes in the second batch.
>
> He ate 3 of the cakes.
>
> How many cakes does Eddie have left?

**2. Major Problem-Solving Approach**

Discuss the problem with the children by asking them the following questions:

*Cakes.*

1 What is the problem about?

*How many cakes does Eddie have left?*

2 What is the question?

*Eddie made 10 cakes, and then he made 9 cakes. He ate 3 of the cakes.*

3 What do you need to know to solve the problem?

*Add the number of cakes Eddie made altogether and take away the number of cakes he ate.*

4 Tell in your own words what you will need to do to solve this problem.

*2*

5 How many steps are in this problem?

*10 + 9 = _____*
*− 3 = _____*

6 Write a number sentence for this problem.

7 What do you think your answer will be?

8 Compute your answer. Is it the same as your estimation?

*Eddie has 16 cakes left.*     9 Give your answer in a sentence.

Follow a similar procedure with Problems 1, 3, and 5 on the student page. Have the children state how many steps are in each problem and the operations that are associated with each of the steps. For Problems 2 and 4, encourage the children to discriminate between the important facts and unimportant facts (unnecessary information).

**ANSWERS**
**(For Student Problems)**

1 Ellen, Rachel, and Debbie would each get 10 stamps.

2 Sam spent $12.

3 Joe has 50¢ left.

4 Peter lives 21 miles from town.

5 Together Julia and Dave worked 42 hours.

*Bonus* Perry ate 5 eggs for breakfast.

**LESSON ⊔-28**                                    Name_____

**SAMPLE PROBLEM**

Eddie made 2 batches of cakes. There were
10 cakes in the first batch and 9 cakes in
the second batch. He ate 3 of the cakes.
How many cakes does Eddie have left?

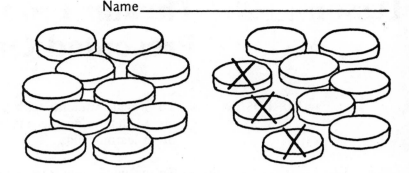

| | |
|---|---|
| **1** Ellen collected 14 stamps, Rachel collected 6 stamps, and Debbie collected 10 stamps. They divided them equally. How many stamps did each get? | **2** Sam went to the store to buy some groceries. Packages of cheese were $2 each, rice was $1 a package, and coffee was $5 a jar. Sam bought 2 jars of coffee and a package of cheese. How much money did he spend? |
| **3** Joe has $1. He bought an apple for 30¢ and candy for 20¢. How much money does Joe have left? | **4** Paul lives 7 miles from town. Joe lives 2 more miles from town than Paul. Peter lives 3 times as far away as Paul. How many miles is Peter from town? |
| **5** Julia worked for 7 hours this week. Dave worked 5 times as many hours as Julia worked. How many hours did they both work altogether? | ***Bonus*** Perry put a dozen eggs in the refrigerator. His brother fried and ate 2 of them for a midnight snack. The next morning, Perry scrambled half of the eggs that were left for his breakfast. How many eggs did he eat for breakfast? |

# Lesson ⊔-29  Theater Problems Presented Orally

PURPOSES
- To provide students with practice in solving orally stated problems. They are to determine the answers without pencil and paper computation or other learning aids.

- To review the major problem-solving approach.

DIRECTIONS

Read each of the problems from student page ⊔-29 to the children twice and ask them to write down the answers only. Remember, no pencil and paper computation is allowed. The students will not need to have copies of the student page for Lesson ⊔-29 before them; however, this may be changed at the option of the teacher. If the children appear to have difficulty with any particular problem, go through the steps of the major problem-solving technique with them. These problems are all based on the theme "Going to the Theater," and there are also some two-step problems and problems containing unnecessary information.

ANSWERS
(For Student Problems)

*Sample*   23 children went to the theater altogether.

1   The play was 2½ hours long.

2   Mary spent 65¢.

3   The children used 5 rows.

4   Sue had $2.50 left.

5   There were 70 people at the play.

*Bonus*   Danny had $1.20 left.

**SAMPLE PROBLEM**

The teacher took the class to the theater

yesterday. There were 10 boys and 13 girls

in the class. How many children went to

the theater altogether?

| | |
|---|---|
| 1  At the theater the children saw a play. There were 5 acts in the play, and each act lasted half an hour. How long was the play? | 2  During the intermission, Mary bought a coke for 40¢ and candy for 25¢. How much money did Mary spend altogether? |
| 3  30 children went to see the play. They sat in rows of 6. How many rows did they take up? | 4  Sue had $5. She paid $2 to see the play, and during the intermission she bought candy for 50¢. How much money did Sue have left? |
| 5  100 people can sit in the theater. There were 20 adults and 50 children at the play. How many people were at the play altogether? | *Bonus*  Danny had $4. He paid $2 to see the play, and during the intermission he bought some popcorn for 45¢ and a cup of orange drink for 35¢. How much money did Danny have left? |

# Lesson ⎕-30    Airport Problems Presented Orally

PURPOSES

- To provide the students with practice in solving orally presented problems.

- To review the major problem-solving approach.

DIRECTIONS

Tell the children that you are going to read some problems aloud to them based on the theme "At the Airport." They can use a pencil and paper to help them to solve the problems; but, unless deemed necessary by the teacher, they do not need to have a copy of the problem sheet for Lesson ⎕-30 before them. Read each of the problems to the children twice and ask them to solve them on their own. If they appear to have difficulty with any particular problem, go through the steps of the major problem-solving approach with them. Included are some two-step problems and problems containing unnecessary information.

ANSWERS
(For Student Problems)

*Sample*   16 of the passengers were men.

1   9 more planes landed in the morning.

2   30 planes were going to Los Angeles.

3   There were 60 people on the plane.

4   There were 33 passengers on the plane.

5   There were 38 suitcases in all.

*Bonus*   $2,500 was paid for all of the tickets.

**SAMPLE PROBLEM**

Chris counted 25 adult passengers

getting off the plane. 9 were women.

How many were men?

| | |
|---|---|
| 1  27 planes landed in the morning. 18 planes landed in the afternoon. How many more planes landed in the morning than in the afternoon? | 2  6 planes were going to San Francisco today. There were 5 times as many planes going to Los Angeles. How many planes were going to Los Angeles today? |
| 3  There were 14 men, 19 women, and 27 children on the plane. How many people were on the plane in all? | 4  There were 16 female passengers and 17 male passengers on another plane. There were also 3 pilots and 5 flight attendants. How many passengers were on the plane? |
| 5  There were 7 men and 8 women on the plane. Each man had 2 suitcases, and each woman had 3 suitcases. How many suitcases were there in all? | *Bonus*  Adult tickets for the airplane flight cost $100 each. Child tickets cost $50 each. There were 12 men, 8 women, 6 boys, and 4 girls on the airplane. How much money was paid to the airline for all of their tickets? |

# Chapter 6

# ORIGINS OF THE MAJOR PROBLEM-SOLVING APPROACH

Classroom teachers have long been aware of the difficulties students encounter with story and word problems. These difficulties result because the students must do more than compute; they must also use the skills of analysis, interpretation, and association to find solutions. Furthermore, story and word problems may be thought of as the bridge between computation and everyday-life math applications. In many instances the word problems are simulations of real-life occurrences.

In recent years the need to have students learn to deal more effectively with problem solving, and specifically word problems, has become a major focus for mathematics instruction. One reason for this emphasis is the conclusion reached by the Elementary School Mathematics Assessment of the Second National Assessment of Educational Progress:

> If it were necessary to single out one area that demands immediate attention, it would clearly be problem solving. At all age levels, and in virtually every content area, performance was extremely low on exercises requiring problem solving or applications of mathematical skills. In general, respondents demonstrated a lack of even the most basic problem-solving skills. Rather than attempting to reason a problem through and figure out what needs to be done to solve the problem, most respondents simply tried to apply a single arithmetic operation to the numbers in the problem. The results indicate that students are not familiar with such basic problem-solving strategies as drawing a picture of a figure described in a problem, substituting smaller numbers in a problem to attempt to find a solution method, or checking the reasonableness of a result.[1]

---

[1] Thomas P. Carpenter, Henry Kepner, Mary Kay Corbitt, Mary Montgomery Lindquist, and Robert E. Reys. Results and Implications of the Second NAEP Mathematics Assessments: Elementary School. *Arithmetic Teacher* 27(8): 47, April 1980.

Early data from the Third National Assessment of Educational Progress again noted that performance on nonroutine problems and on problem solving in general continues to be unacceptably low.[2] As a result of this and other related evidence, the National Council of Teachers of Mathematics recently stated that "the mathematics curriculum should be organized around problem solving."[3] In a similar move, the state of California, in its Mathematics Framework Addendum, has noted that "the Problem Solving/Application Strand has become the overarching theme of all mathematics instruction and is no longer a separate topic."[4] Other states and school districts have reached similar conclusions. Thus it appears that there will be a major focus on problem solving in mathematics education in the foreseeable future.

With a major focus on problem solving, the use of more and varied word problems will undoubtedly result. As such, one concern of teachers and parents becomes that of determining how to help children deal effectively with the many situations that can be portrayed in word problems.

## DECIDING ON A MAJOR APPROACH FOR SOLVING WORD PROBLEMS

For many years, mathematics education researchers have been exploring possible ways to help students deal effectively with story and word problems. Some of their studies have been concerned with specific techniques, such as the use of key words or drawing pictures, while others have involved more inclusive strategies intended for use with any word problem that students might attempt to solve. The emphasis in this section will be upon the use of such major approaches or processes. Pertinent references from the professional literature will be noted; in order that readers may easily obtain them, most will be from sources that are readily available, such as journals and textbooks. The choice of strategies might, of course, be questioned; but in considering practical classroom procedures for word problem solving, the techniques cited herein have been found workable.

In recent years it has been shown that young children can solve word problems. Moser and Carpenter found that six-year-olds, without prior formal instruction, could use a variety of techniques to solve problems such as the following:

Ralph has 4 pieces of gum.

Jeff has 7 pieces of gum.

How many more pieces of gum does Jeff have than Ralph?[5]

---

[2]NAEP Results Released at NCTM's Detroit Meeting. *NCTM News Bulletin.* Reston, Virginia: National Council of Teachers of Mathematics, May 1983, p. 1.

[3]National Council of Teachers of Mathematics. *Recommendations for School Mathematics of the 1980s.* An agenda for action. Reston, Virginia: National Council of Teachers of Mathematics, 1980, p. 2.

[4]California State Board of Education. *Addendum to the Mathematics Framework for California Public Schools, K–12.* Sacramento, California: California State Department of Education, 1980, p. 1.

[5]Jim Moser and Tom Carpenter. Research May Help Tap Natural Problem-Solving Skills. *Wisconsin R and D Center News.* Madison, Wisconsin: Wisconsin Research and Development Center, Fall 1979, p. 6.

While preschool children and students in the early grades are able to deal with such story and word problems, their skills for reasoning through and solving such problems can be improved. To bring about such improvement, Barron suggests the following word problem-solving procedure for use in the early childhood years:

> When teaching students to solve word problems, present a systematic procedure for solving them. This process includes identifying what is to be found and what data are given; determining if the sets involved are to be joined, separated, or compared; modeling the problem situation with objects or pictures (optional as a student's problem solving skills mature); writing and solving the mathematical open sentence; and using the mathematical solution to answer the question in the problem.[6]

Several research studies have investigated the use of similar major problem-solving approaches. In order to determine the effect that an understanding of the processes has upon problem-solving ability, Pace devised a method of instruction in which children from the experimental group were required to read the problem carefully, tell how the problem was to be solved, and tell why a given process was appropriate. Two equated groups took part in this study. Comparisons of the pre- and post-tests showed that the experimental group had statistically significant gains, whereas the control group had only negligible gains. Retention tests after eight weeks showed that both groups maintained their respective gains.[7] These findings were supported by Robinson, who found that good problem solvers used a more formal approach, while poor problem solvers used more different strategies and more trial and error.[8] In a well-controlled study, Wilson examined the following three approaches to problem solving:

1  An action-sequence approach, in which the pupil was taught to "see" or recognize the real or imagined action-sequence of the problem, express the action-sequence in an equation, compute, and check.

2  A wanted-given approach, in which the pupil was taught to recognize the wanted-given structure, express it in an equation, and compute. Focus here was on purposes, ends, and means, and the attributes of what is given and what is wanted.

3  An approach which provided practice only. All subjects used the same study materials, and all three groups were instructed by the researchers.[9]

---

[6]Linda Barron. *Mathematics Experiences for the Early Childhood Years.* Columbus, Ohio: Charles E. Merrill Publishing Co., 1979, p. 280.

[7]Angela Pace. Understanding and the Ability to Solve Problems. *Arithmetic Teacher* 8(5): 226–233, May 1961.

[8]Mary L. Robinson. An Investigation of Problem Solving Behavior and Cognitive and Affective Characteristics of Good and Poor Problem Solvers in Sixth Grade Math. *Dissertation Abstracts* 33: 5620, 1973.

[9]John W. Wilson. The Role of Structure in Problem Solving. *Arithmetic Teacher* 14(6): 487–88, October 1967.

The findings reported by Wilson included the following:

1 Those students of the wanted-given group, which emphasized the attributes of the arithmetical operation, showed significant gains over the others in correct answer, correct operation, and growth.

2 The action-sequence program produced no statistically significant improvement.[10]

In a somewhat similar study, Jerman considered whether a method that teaches general problem-solving skills and assumes transfer to specific disciplines such as mathematics would be more effective than a modified wanted-given program designed specifically to teach problem solving in mathematics. Initial analyses revealed slight differences in favor of the modified wanted-given procedure, but none of these were significant. However, subsequent analyses did find that students taught the modified wanted-given method used correct procedures to solve post-test word problems significantly more often than the other groups.[11] Lee suggested that in guiding young children to successful problem solving, the children need to (1) understand the problem, (2) make a plan, (3) carry out the plan, and (4) look back.[12] LeBlanc noted that teachers can help students deal successfully with textbook-type story problems by systematically having them Tell, Show, Solve, and Check.[13] Furthermore, in reference to research on problem solving, Suydam indicates that teachers should "teach children a variety of problem-solving strategies plus an overall plan for how to go about problem solving."[14]

Rincon and Ryan tried the following word problem-solving procedures with students in Kindergarten through Grade 6:

1 A major problem-solving approach, which used elements of the wanted-given method in a semiformal analysis setting. In this approach the students in the Experimental Group were helped to analyze and solve word problems by determining and verbally stating the following:

   a Main idea

   b Question

   c Important facts

   d Relationship sentence

   e Equation

---

[10]*Ibid.*, p. 496.

[11]Max Jerman. Individualized Instruction in Problem Solving in Elementary School Mathematics. *Journal for Research in Mathematics Education* 4(1): 6–19, January 1973.

[12]Kil S. Lee. Guiding Young Children in Successful Problem Solving. *Arithmetic Teacher* 29(5): 16, January 1982.

[13]John F. LeBlanc. Teaching Textbook Story Problems. *Arithmetic Teacher* 29(6): 52, February 1982.

[14]Marilyn N. Suydam. Update on Research on Problem Solving: Implications for Classroom Teaching. *Arithmetic Teacher* 29(6): 56–60, February 1982.

f  Estimation

g  Computation

h  Answer sentence

The steps from this major problem-solving approach were followed together with a series of support techniques (such as using manipulatives, drawing pictures, etc.).

2  A Practice Group used the same set of lessons but did not receive directed instruction in either the major problem-solving approach or the support techniques.

3  A Control Group followed their regular textbook program.[15]

On the basis of their findings, Rincon and Ryan concluded:

1  The major approach and the supporting techniques were successful in Kindergarten through Grade 6, especially in Grades 1, 2, and 6.

2  Intensive practice in problem solving is not sufficient to increase problem-solving ability without instruction in specific techniques.[16]

Therefore it would appear that teaching students to solve mathematics word problems with a modified wanted-given approach is advisable. Furthermore, using such a procedure in a semiformal analysis setting is preferred. The authors of this book termed this combination of word problem-solving procedures the *major problem-solving approach*. Specific instructions on how to use this approach are found in Chapter 1 of this book, and teacher lesson plans and student word problem pages based on it are given in Chapters 2 through 5.

**CHOOSING SUPPORTING TECHNIQUES**

Much of the literature indicates specific supporting procedures that teachers should use when helping children with certain types of story or word problems. It is suggested that, when appropriate, these support techniques be used along with the major problem-solving approach. For example, Riedesel noted that

> Greater use should be made of such specific procedures as writing the number question, use of drawings and diagrams, pupil formulation of problems, orally presented problems, and using problems without numerals.[17]

---

[15] Jane C. Rincon and Constance A. Ryan. Problem Solving Techniques for Elementary School Mathematics. Unpublished Master's Thesis, California State University, Chico, California, 1978, pp. 35–48.

[16] *Ibid.*, pp. 52, 55, and 77.

[17] C. A. Riedesel. Verbal Problem Solving: Suggestions for Improving Instruction. *Arithmetic Teacher* 11(5): 316, May 1964.

Among the many studies relating to supporting problem-solving techniques are the following:

**Vocabulary Instruction**

Faulk and Landry devised a systematic approach to problem solving in which vocabulary was emphasized at the beginning of each class period. This was followed by:

1 Talking or thinking through the problem situation.

2 Drawing a diagram of the problem situation.

3 Estimating the answer.[18]

Vanderlinde, Dahmus, and Richardson found that pupils who studied quantitative vocabulary by direct study techniques did obtain higher mean achievement scores in arithmetic problem solving and in arithmetic concepts than pupils who did not study quantitative vocabulary in this way.[19,20,21]

In terms of practical suggestions for use with students, Barnett, Sowder and Vos suggest:

> Some words—such as sum, total, decrease, and difference—can provide clues to help learners translate the data contained in the problem statement into equations. . . . Unfortunately, the same term may not always indicate the same operation or procedure in different contexts. . . . Perhaps the best method is to have children look for the potential key words as they read through the problem. During a second reading, they can use contextual clues to help determine which of the identified words are actually operational or procedural indicators.[22]

**Reading Instruction in a Mathematical Context**

There are different points of view regarding the use of formal reading instruction as a technique to improve students' word problem-solving abilities. Earle indicates that success with mathematics word problems depends to a great extent on success in reading:

---

[18] Charles J. Faulk and Thomas R. Laudry. An Approach to Problem Solving. *Arithmetic Teacher* 8(4): 157–60, April 1961.

[19] Louis F. Vanderlinde. Does the Study of Quantitative Vocabulary Improve Problem Solving? *Elementary School Journal* 65: 143–52, December 1964.

[20] Maurice E. Dahmus. How to Teach Verbal Problems. *School Science and Mathematics* 70: 121–38, February 1970.

[21] Lloyd Richardson. The Role of Strategies for Teaching Pupils to Solve Verbal Problems. *Arithmetic Teacher* 22(5): 414–21, May 1975.

[22] Jeffery Barnett, Larry Sowder, and Kenneth E. Vos. Textbook Problems: Supplementing and Understanding Them. *Problem Solving in School Mathematics*. 1980 Yearbook. Reston, Virginia: National Council of Teachers of Mathematics, pp. 100–101.

The solution of word problems is one of the most sophisticated of all tasks in mathematics, at least from the reading point of view. It is here that the reader must perform accurately all the previous levels of reading—perceiving symbols, attaching literal meaning, and analyzing relationships—and extend that knowledge toward the correct or creative solution of a mathematical problem, actual or simulated.[23]

Knifong and Holtan acknowledged the fact that when a child cannot read a word problem, he or she cannot solve it; but they were concerned with whether poor reading skills typically contribute to failure with word problems. According to their results, "it is difficult to imagine that poor reading ability accounts for more than ten percent of the erred problems."[24] Thus their "recommendation for teachers is (1) help students develop computational skills, and (2) do not expect work on reading skills (which may be valuable in its own right) to correct word problem difficulties."[25]

While it is difficult to assess the impact of reading ability on the problem-solving process, Barnett, Sowder and Vos indicate that

> It is clear, however, that many children with poor language skills never reach the stage of understanding the problem. By systematically providing experiences to help them develop language-processing skills in the area of mathematics, the teacher can help children improve their ability in this crucial area of problem solving.[26]

Finally, in an article summarizing recent research on problem solving, Suydam indicates that "there is also evidence that instruction on reading skills can lead to higher problem solving scores."[27] She does go on to note, however, that "to equate problem-solving difficulty with reading difficulty appears to be too great a simplification. To help children interpret the words in a problem is, however, of vital concern."[28]

**Instruction in Writing Equations**

Arnold discovered that a child's ability to express problem relationships as number sentences was highly related to problem-solving ability.[29] Schonherr

---

[23]Richard A. Earle. *Teaching Reading and Mathematics.* Reading Aid Series. Newark, Delaware: International Reading Association, 1976, p. 49.

[24]J. Dan Knifong and Boyd D. Holtan. A Search for Reading Difficulties Among Erred Word Problems. *Journal for Research in Mathematics Education* 8(3): 229, May 1977.

[25]*Ibid.*, p. 230.

[26]Barnett, Sowder, and Vos, *op. cit.*, p. 103.

[27]Suydam, *op. cit.*, p. 59.

[28]*Ibid.*

[29]William R. Arnold. Knowledge of Vocabulary, Ability to Formulate Equations, and Ability to Solve Verbal Problems: An Investigation of Relationships. *Dissertation Abstracts* 29A: 2031–32, 1969.

described her method of teaching children how to write equations for "story problems" as follows:

1  Ask the children to solve a simple problem in their usual way.

2  Ask the children to combine all their steps into one equation. (This involved transferring the old-fashioned "vertical" way of recording to the new "horizontal" way.)[30]

## Instruction in Making Diagrams and Drawings

Spitzer and Flournoy investigated and analyzed examples of classroom procedures for improving problem solving. One such procedure was for the children to draw the problem situation. The teacher then asked them questions about their drawings. The investigators recommended that this procedure be used to help supplement the usual program.[31] Nelson also found that students' drawing of diagrams improves problem-solving performance on problems that readily lend themselves to this technique.[32]

## Encouraging Children to Write Their Own Problems

Davidson maintained that the "language-experience" approach to teaching children to solve story problems is one method that helps to overcome the problems of low reading comprehension, lack of experience with the problem situation, and unfamiliarity with the language of the problem.[33] Keil also found that pupils who wrote and solved their own problems were superior in arithmetic problem-solving ability to pupils who have had the usual textbook experiences in problem solving.[34] Finally, Wirtz and Kahn noted that

> When children learn mathematics by making up their own stories involving numbers and other mathematical notions, they can transfer these skills more easily to applications in books or tests as well as to situations requiring computation in daily life.[35]

---

[30] Betty Schonherr. Writing Equations for Story Problems. *Arithmetic Teacher* 15(10): 562–63, October 1968.

[31] Herbert F. Spitzer and Frances Flournoy. Developing Facility in Solving Word Problems. *Arithmetic Teacher* 3(11): 177–82, November 1951.

[32] Glenn T. Nelson. The Effects of Diagram Drawing and Translation on Pupils' Mathematics Problem Solving Performance. *Dissertation Abstracts* 35: 4149, 1975.

[33] James E. Davidson. The Language Experience Approach to Story Problems. *Arithmetic Teacher* 25(10): 28, October 1977.

[34] Gloria E. Keil. Writing and Solving Original Problems as a Means of Improving Verbal Arithmetic Problem Solving Ability. *Dissertation Abstracts* 25: 7109–10, 1965.

[35] Robert W. Wirtz and Emily Kahn. Another Look at Applications in Elementary School Mathematics. *Arithmetic Teacher* 30(1): 21, September 1982.

**Using Problems without Numbers, Problems with Unnecessary Information, and Problems with Insufficient Data**

Klas encouraged the use of problems without numbers to challenge the more able student. He suggested that in a problem such as "How much will a vacation cost the family?" the teacher should only give information that is asked for by the children. Klas also felt that this type of problem lends itself particularly to individual differences.[36] Talton recommended that children be given experience with verbal problems that contain unnecessary data, insufficient data, and no numbers in order to improve problem-solving ability.[37]

**Using Problems Related to a Particular Theme**

Sinner suggested that problems should be formulated that use the direct experience of the children or are related to areas that are of particular interest to different age groups.[38]

**SUMMARY**

Much of the research and expert opinion indicates that a major problem-solving approach does help children to work successfully through and solve mathematics word problems. A series of support techniques (such as drawing diagrams and writing their own problems) can also be an aid to understanding specific types of problems. When children are taught how to use these procedures together and then provided with ample word problems for practice, they have a greater chance of becoming successful word problem solvers.

In this book the authors have designated a major problem-solving approach and a series of support techniques that teachers and/or parents may use with young children. (See Chapter 1 for details.) They have also provided a series of problem-solving lessons that are appropriate for beginners, and Grades 1, 2, and 3. (See Chapters 2 through 5.) By the time children have completed the lessons appropriate to their level, they will have gained a knowledge of problem-solving situations and the necessary skills to be better able to deal with them.

[36]Walter L. Klas. Problems Without Numbers. *Arithmetic Teacher* 8(1): 19–20, January 1961.

[37]Carolyn F. Talton. An Investigation of Selected Mental, Mathematical, Reading, and Personality Assessments as Predictors of High Achievers in Sixth Grade Mathematical Verbal Problem Solving. *Dissertation Abstracts* 34A: 1008–09, 1973.

[38]C. Sinner. The Problem of Problem Solving. *Arithmetic Teacher* 6(4): 158–59, April 1959.

# SUGGESTED REFERENCES

Arnold, William R. 1969. Knowledge of vocabulary, ability to formulate equations, and ability to solve verbal problems: An investigation of relationships. *Dissertation Abstracts* 29A: 2031-32.

Bana, Jack, and Doyal Nelson. 1978. Distractors in nonverbal mathematics problems. *Journal for Research in Mathematics Education* 9(1): 55-61.

Barnett, Jeffery, Larry Sowder, and Kenneth E. Vos. 1980. Textbook problems: Supplementing and understanding them. *Problem solving in school mathematics.* Reston, Virginia: National Council of Teachers of Mathematics.

Barron, Linda. 1979. *Mathematics experiences for the early childhood years.* Columbus, Ohio: Charles E. Merrill Publishing Co.

Brush, Lorelei. 1978. Preschool children's knowledge of addition and subtraction. *Journal for Research in Mathematics Education* 8(1): 44-52.

California State Board of Education. 1980. Addendum to the mathematics framework for California public schools, K-12. Sacramento, California: California State Department of Education.

Carpenter, Thomas P., Terrance C. Colburn, Robert E. Reys, and James W. Wilson. 1976. Notes from national assessment: Word problems. *Arithmetic Teacher* 25(9): 389-93.

Carpenter, Thomas P., Henry Kepner, Mary Kay Corbitt, Mary Montgomery Lindquist, and Robert E. Reys. 1980. Results and implications of the second NAEP mathematics assessments: Elementary school. *Arithmetic Teacher* 27(8): 10-12 and 44-47.

Dahmus, Maurice E. 1970. How to teach verbal problems. *School Science and Mathematics* 70: 121-38.

Davidson, James E. 1977. The language experience approach to story problems. *Arithmetic Teacher* 25(1): 28.

Earle, Richard A. 1976. *Teaching reading and mathematics.* Reading aid series. Newark, Delaware: International Reading Association.

Faulk, Charles J., and Thomas R. Landry. 1961. An approach to problem solving. *Arithmetic Teacher* 8(4): 157-60.

Freeman, George F. 1973. Reading and mathematics. *Arithmetic Teacher* 23(2): 523-29.

Heddens, James W., and Kenneth J. Smith. 1964. The readability of elementary mathematics books. *Arithmetic Teacher* 3(2): 466-68.

Hendrickson, A. Dean. 1979. An inventory of mathematical thinking done by incoming first grade children. *Journal for Research in Mathematics Education* 9(1): 7-22.

Jerman, Max. 1973. Individualized instruction in problem solving in elementary school mathematics. *Journal for Research in Mathematics Education* 4(1): 6-19.

Keil, Gloria E. 1965. Writing and solving original problems as a means of improving verbal arithmetic problem solving ability. *Dissertation Abstracts* 25: 7109-10.

Klas, Walter L. 1961. Problems without numbers. *Arithmetic Teacher* 8(1): 19-20.

Knifong, J. Dan, and Boyd D. Holtan. 1977. A search for reading difficulties among erred word problems. *Journal for Research in Mathematics Education* 8(3): 227-30.

Krulik, Stephen, and Jesse A. Rudnick. 1980. *Problem solving: A handbook for teachers.* Boston: Allyn and Bacon, Inc.

LeBlanc, John F. 1982. Teaching textbook story problems. *Arithmetic Teacher* 29(6): 52-54.

Lee, Kil S. 1982. Guiding young children in successful problem solving. *Arithmetic Teacher* 29(5): 15-17.

Liedtke, Werner. 1977. The young child as a problem solver. *Arithmetic Teacher* 24(4): 333-38.

Moser, Jim, and Tom Carpenter. 1979. Research may help tap natural problem solving skills. *Wisconsin R and D Center News.* Madison, Wisconsin: Wisconsin Research and Development Center.

NAEP results released at NCTM's Detroit meeting. 1983. *NCTM News Bulletin.* Reston, Virginia: National Council of Teachers of Mathematics.

National Council of Teachers of Mathematics. 1980. *Recommendations for school mathematics of the 1980s.* An agenda for action. Reston, Virginia: National Council of Teachers of Mathematics.

Nelson, Glenn T. 1975. The effects of diagram drawing and translation on pupils' mathematics problem solving performance. *Dissertation Abstracts* 35: 4149.

Overholt, James L. 1978. *Dr. Jim's elementary math prescriptions.* Glenview, Illinois: Scott, Foresman and Co. (Goodyear Books).

Pace, Angela. 1961. Understanding the ability to solve problems. *Arithmetic Teacher* 8(5): 226-33.

Payne, Joseph N. (ed.). 1975. *Mathematics learning in early childhood.* Reston, Virginia: National Council of Teachers of Mathematics.

Richardson, Lloyd. 1975. The role of strategies for teaching pupils to solve verbal problems. *Arithmetic Teacher* 22(5): 414-21.

Riedesel, C. Alan. 1969. Problem solving: Some suggestions from research. *Arithmetic Teacher* 17(5): 54-55.

Riedesel, C. Alan. 1964. Verbal problem solving: Suggestions for improving instruction. *Arithmetic Teacher* 11(5): 312-16.

Rincon, Jane C., and Constance A. Ryan. 1978. Problem solving techniques for elementary school mathematics. Unpublished Master's Thesis, California State University, Chico, California.

Robinson, H. Alan. 1975. *Teaching reading and study strategies: The content areas.* Boston: Allyn and Bacon, Inc.

Robinson, Mary L. 1973. An investigation of problem solving behavior and cognitive and affective characteristics of good and poor problem solvers in sixth grade math. *Dissertation Abstracts* 33: 5620.

Schonherr, Betty. 1968. Writing equations for story problems. *Arithmetic Teacher* 15(10): 562-63.

Sinner, C. 1959. The problem of problem solving. *Arithmetic Teacher* 6(4): 158-59.

Spitzer, Herbert F., and Frances Flournoy. 1951. Developing facility in solving word problems. *Arithmetic Teacher* 3(11): 177-82.

Steffe, Leslie P. 1970. Differential performance of first-grade children when solving arithmetic problems. *Journal for Research in Mathematics Education* 1(3): 144-61.

Steffe, Leslie P., and David C. Johnson. 1971. Problem solving performances of first grade children. *Journal for Research in Mathematics Education* 1(1): 2 and 50-64.

Suydam, Marilyn N. 1982. Update on research on problem solving: Implications for classroom teaching. *Arithmetic Teacher* 29(6): 56-60.

Suydam, Marilyn N., and J. Fred Weaver. 1977. Research on problem solving: Implications for elementary school classrooms. *Arithmetic Teacher* 25(2): 40-42.

Talton, Carolyn F. 1973. An investigation of selected mental, mathematical, reading, and personality assessments as predictors of high achievers in sixth grade mathematical verbal problem solving. *Dissertation Abstracts* 34A: 1008-09.

Vanderlinde, Louis F. 1964. Does the study of quantitative vocabulary improve problem solving? *Elementary School Journal* 65: 143-52.

Wilson, John W. 1967. The role of structure in problem solving. *Arithmetic Teacher* 14(6): 486-97.

Wirtz, Robert W., and Emily Kahn. 1982. Another look at applications in elementary school mathematics. *Arithmetic Teacher* 30(1): 21-24.

Wisner, Robert J. (n.d.) *Problem solving strategies for elementary mathematics.* Glenview, Illinois: Scott, Foresman and Co.

Zweng, Marilyn J. 1979. The problem of solving story problems. *Arithmetic Teacher* 27(1): 2-3.

# INDEX

| PROBLEM SOLVING TECHNIQUE | BEGINNERS | GRADE 1 | GRADE 2 | GRADE 3 |
|---|---|---|---|---|
| Diagrams | | 114 | 141, 157, 161 | 203, 209, 212, 251, 254, 267 |
| Tables | | | 164 | 215, 257 |
| Charts and Graphs | 61 | 111 | 169 | 219, 260 |
| Estimating | 49, 53, 64, 67, 69 | 89, 92, 95, 99, 102, 105, 108, 114, 122 | 132, 141, 151, 157, 161, 164, 168, 173 | 184, 187, 193, 206, 209, 212, 215, 219, 226, 229, 232, 235, 238, 241, 245, 248, 251, 254, 257, 260, 267, 270 |
| Writing Our Own Problems | 47, 61, 72 | 118, 120 | 177 | 223 |
| Problem Themes | 42, 44, 47, 52, 61, 72 | 95, 99, 111, 118 | 147, 168 | 199, 215, 217, 219, 238, 241, 257, 260, 264, 270, 272 |
| Two-Step Problems | | | 173 | 267, 270 |
| Problems with Unneeded Information | | | | 267, 270 |